HOW TO USE THIS GUIDE

In this guide, the text of the European Commission Code of Practice on measures to combat sexual harassment is printed in bold. Paragraph numbers in respect of the paragraphs of the Code of Practice have been introduced in order to make reference easier.

The authors' commentary on the Code of Practice and the issues it raises is printed in ordinary type immediately following the relevant paragraph of the Code of Practice.

Examples of interesting initiatives taken in Member States appear after the commentary in respect of the relevant paragraph, beginning with paragraph 1.3.

FOREWORD

Women in the European Community have been going out to work in ever greater numbers over the past decade. They have become an indispensable part of the workforce, and despite the threat of recession, look set to stay that way in the long term.

But many still have to cope with the extra strain of life in workplaces where they are vulnerable in particular to insidious kinds of attention — because they are women.

Unwanted personal attention or sexually-motivated behaviour that embarrasses a colleague is hardly a new phenomenon, but it is only recently that business and unions have started to take it seriously.

Turning a blind eye to sexual harassment costs time and money. Organizations should think seriously about the cumulative cost of replacing staff affected, paying sick leave to employees who miss work because of stress, and the implications of reduced individual and group productivity — all expensive drains on the morale and efficiency of workplace teams.

We can add to that the costs of investigating and defending complaints, legal costs, as well as the business cost of losing public goodwill after adverse publicity.

Awareness of the potentially disruptive dynamics involved in sexual harassment may help all involved in personnel issues to account for otherwise inexplicable deteriorations in performance, and to act in good time to restore optimal working relations.

European Community ministers put their weight behind wide-spread efforts to make workplaces more congenial for both sexes with their May 1990 Resolution on the protection of dignity in the workplace. The Commission has played its part with a Recommendation and a Code of Practice for action on the issue.

This Guide illustrating the Code of Practice on combating sexual harassment at work is intended as a practical, pragmatic handbook. It brings together extracts from policy statements, equal opportunities programmes, laws and court cases — real examples of the efforts people are currently making to eliminate the problem.

We hope it will help employers, unions, employees' representatives and women's organisations plan their strategy to increase awareness about unacceptable behaviour to prevent it happening, and to deal with problems constructively if and when they do arise.

Agnès HUBERT
Head of Equal Opportunities Unit

6

CONTENTS

1. INTRODUCTION

1.1. This Code of Practice is issued in accordance with the Resolution of the Council of Ministers on the protection of the dignity of women and men at work[1] and to accompany the Commission's Recommendation on this issue.

The Council Resolution of 29 May 1990, the Commission Recommendation of 27 November 1991 and the Council Declaration of 29 November 1991 are reproduced as an appendix to this Guide. These instruments represent the latest stage in growing awareness throughout the Community of the problem of sexual harassment at work.

The Council Resolution of 29 May 1990 on the protection of the dignity of women and men at work called on the Commission to draw up a Code of Practice. In the event the Code was annexed to a Commission Recommendation.

The Commission Recommendation and the Code are not legally binding in themselves, but the European Court has held (Case 322/88) that National Courts are bound to take the Recommendation into consideration in order to decide disputes submitted to them, in particular where they clarify the interpretation of national decisions adopted in order to implement them or where they are designed to supplement binding Community measures.

1.2. Its purpose is to give practical guidance to employers, trade unions, and employees on the protection of the dignity of women and men at work. The Code is intended to be applicable in both the public and the private sector and employers are encouraged to follow the recommendations contained in the Code in a way which is appropriate to the size and structure of their organization. It may be particularly relevant for small and medium-sized

---

[1] OJ C 157, 27.6.1990, p. 3.

enterprises to adapt some of the practical steps to their specific needs.

In many cases, smaller organizations will have to adapt the recommendations made in the Code of Practice to what is practicable given their resources. Consideration should be given to cooperating with other organizations in the same industry or locality, where appropriate.

'Smaller firms are more limited when it comes to the more important elements, such as the appointment of a company confidential counsellor, a complaints commission or the involvement of a works council and/or a member of the personnel department (...)

The limited resources make the role played by the management all the more important (...) The relationship between the management and the workforce is relatively close and everyone knows one another. As a rule, the management has a good idea of what goes on in the company and is consequently in a better position to take direct action in cases of sexual harassment.

In terms of policy development, small(er) firms would be best advised to participate in existing forms of cooperation with other companies. The printing industry has opted for an approach at sector level. A detailed provision has been included in the collective labour agreement and a common intrasectorial information brochure published. Similarly, the appointment of a confidential counsellor, the creation of a complaints procedure and a complaints commission with the same sphere of activity as the collective labour agreement could merit consideration, as could a combined approach to providing information and training. Take the employers and employees in the catering sector, for example. They have provided for the appointment of a central confidential counsellor in the collective labour agreement.'

Sexual harassement, Drs I.M de Vries, Commissie Ontwikkeling Bedrijven (Company Development Committee) / Sociaal Economische Raad (Socio-Economic Council), **the Netherlands.**

1.3. The aim is to ensure that sexual harassment does not occur and, if it does occur, to ensure that adequate procedures are readily available to deal with the problem and prevent its recurrence. The Code thus seeks to encourage the development and implementation of policies and practices which establish working environments free of sexual harassment and in which women and men respect one another's human integrity.

The Code recommends that employers adopt a 'twin-track' strategy. Action is needed to protect employees against the risk of sexual harassment at work and action also is needed to provide mechanisms to deal with the problem when it arises. Note, however, that the action required to achieve each goal has a different emphasis. In order to minimize the risk of sexual harassment occurring, training and communication strategies are needed. Once an incident of sexual harassment has taken place, effective complaints and counselling procedures should be available.

1.4. The expert report carried out on behalf of the Commission found that sexual harassment is a serious problem for many working women in the European Community[1] and research in Member States has proven beyond doubt that sexual harassment at work is not an isolated phenomenon. On the contrary, it is clear that for millions of women in the European Community, sexual harassment is an unpleasant and unavoidable part of their working lives. Men, too, may suffer sexual harassment and should, of course, have the same rights as women to the protection of their dignity.

It is not always recognised that sexual harassment is a problem. Surveys carried out in almost all the Member States show that it is a problem in every country. The results vary according to the precise questions asked, according to how sexual harassment is defined, and according to general awareness of the problem. For

---

[1] *The dignity of women at work: A report on the problem of sexual harassment in the Member States of the European Communities,* October 1987, by Michael Rubenstein (ISBN 92-825-8764-9).

11

example, the term 'sexual harassment' itself is not always understood. Therefore, fewer women will say that they have experienced 'sexual harassment' than will say that they have experienced 'unwanted sexual advances'. What the research does establish is that the proportion of women in each Member State experiencing the behaviour is sufficiently high as to make it highly likely that sexual harassment at work is a problem for every organization.

The research also documents that a smaller, but none the less significant, number of men complain of sexual harassment at work. Men can be sexually harassed by women and by other men. These findings are so persistent that they cannot be dismissed. It is true that the form which sexual harassment of men by women takes normally differs from harassment by men of women. It is much more likely to take the form of excessive teasing or bullying than of requests for sexual favours. Nevertheless, the research does not support the view that sexual harassment of women bears no resemblance to sexual harassment of men. On the contrary, as indicated below, women and men who are most likely to be sexually harassed share the common feature that they are likely to have a characteristic which makes them comparatively powerless and vulnerable to harassment.

'Of the women questioned, 93 % report first-hand experiences at work of the 'occurrences' mentioned in the questionnaire, stating that they have experienced at least one of these situations (regardless of whether they themselves classify these as harassment). Deducting from this information the entries relating to the three types of conduct not considered by the majority as sexual harassment, the following results are obtained:

Of the women asked, 72 % have experienced situations at work which the majority (at least 73 % of those asked) classified as sexual harassment. More than two-thirds of the women we asked had therefore been affected at work by situations (potentially) characterizable as sexual harassment.'

Sexual harassment at work, M. Holzbecher *et al.*, Dortmund Institute for Social Research, Ministry of Women and Youth, **Germany.**

'In accordance with the answers to question..., which accurately represents the occurrence of cases of sexual harassment for the total population, 65.9% of those asked claim never to have been the recipient of sexual harassment, 19.1% have seldom been so, 9.4% sometimes and 5.7% often.'

Research into sexual harassment in the workplace, Ligia Amancio and Maria Luisa Pedroso Lima, Portuguese Institute of Work and Enterprise Science, **Portugal.**

'Assessment of the phenomenon of harassment

Out of all French men and women aged 18 and above, 21% had first-hand experience of harassment and 9% of working women have experienced highly or moderately unpleasant situations. A further 6% of women have witnessed harassment. Also, 6% of men have witnessed harassment.'

Louis Harris poll, **France.**

'19% of the male participants in the written survey feel they have been sexually harassed. They mention similar experiences to the women.

Because the male victims are seldom dependent on the harasser, the experience cuts less deep and is felt less as a burden. Male victims are more successful in protecting themselves from further harassment. They report far less mental and physical damage, as well as less negative consequences for their professional situation, than the female victims.'

Sexual harassment at work, M. Holzbecher *et al.*, Dortmund Institute for Social Research, Ministry of Youth, Family, Women and Health, **Germany.**

'The worker alleges that during his employment he was sexually harassed by a company director (name supplied to the Court). The instances alleged included crude language and offensive comments and actions of a sexual nature. The worker claims that these discriminatory working conditions were both demeaning and distressing to him and ultimately resulted in his dismissal.

The worker gave details of specific incidents which occurred between October 1990 and March 1991. These incidents included being asked by the director to go to the chemist for condoms or menstrual pads. He was also subjected to a "sex survey" by the director in which she asked him intimate and embarrassing questions (details supplied to the court). All these incidents created a hostile and discriminatory working environment for the worker.

... the Court is satisfied that the complaint is well founded and that the complainant was discriminated against in contravention of the Employment Equality Act 1977 and that this discrimination led to his parents' intervention and his consequent dismissal from his employment.

The Court will therefore make an order directing the respondent company to pay to the complainant the sum of IRL 1 000 compensation.'

A company v *A worker*, 22 July 1992, **Ireland.**

1.5. **Some specific groups are particularly vulnerable to sexual harassment. Research in several Member States, which documents the link between the risk of sexual harassment and the recipient's perceived vulnerability, suggests that divorced and separated women, young women and new entrants to the labour market and those with irregular or precarious employment contracts, women in non-traditional jobs, women with disabilities, lesbians and women from racial minorities are disproportionately at risk. Gay men and young men are also vulnerable to harassment. It is undeniable that harassment on grounds of sexual orientation undermines the dignity at work of those affected and it is impossible to regard such harassment as appropriate workplace behaviour.**

(i) The study conducted on behalf of the Commission on Women and Labour in Belgium found that unmarried, divorced or separated women were at special risk of harassment.

14

(ii) A study undertaken by the Women's Institute in Spain found that 90% of young women in their first jobs had experienced harassment.

(iii) A study carried out by the Leeds Trade Union and Community Resource and Information Centre in the UK found that 96% of the women in 'non-traditional' women's occupations surveyed had experienced harassment.

(iv) The UK advice and support group Women Against Sexual Harassment report that in 1991 it assisted 6 232 people. Of the clients 27% were Asian or black women and a total of 43% were from minority ethnic groups in the UK (including workers from other EEC countries).

(v) WASH also reports that 24% of its complaints were brought by lesbians or gay men and 15% by women or men with disabilities.

Sexual harassment which is linked to racism or to sexual orientation is still sexual harassment. Sexual abuse or sexually-explicit remarks based on racist sterotypes should be regarded as sexual harassement under this code. And both heterosexuals and homosexuals must be protected from sexual harassement.

'At the time of harassment, recipients tend to be 20-30 years old, unmarried, childless and relatively new to the company. Of these, 66%, that is two-thirds, had been working at the company less than three years when the harassment occurred. Superiors, compared to other groups of persons, are more likely to harass women who have been working for less than one year. The women reported a conspicuously large number of cases of harassment during their vocational training, more than every fifth case of harassment particularly remembered by women falling into this category. Just as many women report having been in temporary employment at the time of harassment; at any rate 18% had been at the company for only six months at this point, being therefore presumably still in their trial period.'

15

Sexual harassment at work, M. Holzbecher *et al.*, Dortmund Institute for Social Research, Ministry of Youth, Family, Women and Health, **Germany.**

'Lesbian and gay workers are often subjected to harassment from management and co-workers
...

The harassment can be verbal, such as unwanted personal questions and remarks, offensive jokes, innuendo and malicious gossip. A lesbian or gay worker may be isolated or "frozen out" by co-workers. In extreme cases a person may be physically attacked.
...

Many lesbian and gay workers are forced to conceal their sexuality which has serious consequences for their health, work performance and promotion prospects.'

'Lesbian and gay rights in the workplace, guidelines for negotiators', Irish Congress of Trade Unions, **Ireland.**

'Our survey found that Asian and black women were more likely to experience sexual harassment than their white counterparts, and that racist language or stereotypes informed the experience of harassment in over 50% of these cases. The group of women most frequently affected (often by more serious forms of harassment) also appeared to be less likely to receive worthwhile help from their employers as a source of potential help. Of white women, 59% thought that employers would be a helpful ally as opposed to only 20% of Asian or black women.'

'Racially explicit sexual harassment', Women Against Sexual Harassment, **United Kingdom.**

1.6. **Sexual harassment pollutes the working environment and can have a devastating effect upon the health, confidence, morale and performance of those affected by it. The anxiety and stress produced by sexual harassment commonly leads to those subjected to it taking time off work due to sickness, being less efficient at work, or leaving their job to seek work elsewhere.**

Employees often suffer both the adverse consequences of the harassment itself and short- and long-term damage to their employment prospects if they are forced to change jobs. Sexual harassment may also have a damaging impact on employees not themselves the object of unwanted behaviour but who are witness to it or have a knowledge of the unwanted behaviour.

It is now well documented by research in many countries as well as by experience of dealing with victims that sexual harassment can result in damaging emotional, physical and work-performance stress, as the examples below indicate.

'Sexual harassment

(i) may make you strained and angry;
(ii) may cause depressions;
(iii) may make you suffer from sleeplessness and stress-related symptoms like headaches, skin problems, digestion problems, inflammation of the bladder, etc.

Sexual harassment

(i) affects your workmanship;
(ii) may affect your promotion possibilities;
(iii) may affect your confidence in your work;
(iv) may mean that you are forced to resign or that you are dismissed.'

'How to deal with sexual harassment', Clerical Workers Union (HK), **Denmark.**

'Sexual harassment may entail dramatic consequences for the person exposed to it: a lack of concentration in professional activities, physical or psychological impairment. It may also entail loss of job or a promotion. It is not of benefit to anyone. It creates an unpleasant work environment, it harms good relations and through this the proper operation of the firm or service and the efficiency of work.'

'Sex collègue? Ex-collègue', Cabinet of the Secretary of State for Social Emancipation, **Belgium.**

1.7. There are also adverse consequences arising from sexual harassment for employers. It has a direct impact on the profitability of the enterprise where staff take sick leave or resign their posts because of sexual harassment, and on the economic efficiency of the enterprise where employees' productivity is reduced by having to work in a climate in which individuals' integrity is not respected.

Permitting sexual harassment does not make good business sense. According to the United States Merit System Protection Board's report *Sexual Harassment In the Federal Government: An Update (1988),* sexual harassment cost the US Federal Government an estimated $267 million during the period May 1985 to May 1987. These figures represent the cost of replacing employees who missed work, and reduced individual and group productivity.

'Sexual harassment imposes costs on the organization in the form of high staff turnover, reduced productivity, lowered staff morale, absenteeism, sickness, health and safety risks, etc., which impede efficiency and reduce profitability.'

Tolerating sexual harassment is inconsistent with the aims of "Quality through people". The Board is anxious to work with its employees towards creating a working environment where all employees are treated with dignity and respect'.

Policy on sexual harassment, British Railways Board, **United Kingdom.**

1.8. In general terms, sexual harassment is an obstacle to the proper integration of women into the labour market and the Commission is committed to encouraging the development of comprehensive measures to improve such integration.[1]

---

[1] Third Action Programme on equal opportunities for women and men, 1991 to 1995, COM(90) 449, 6.11.1990.

Women who are the victims of sexual harassment often suffer a double penalty. They suffer the adverse consequences of the harassment itself. They may also suffer long-term damage to their career prospects if they change jobs as a result of the harassment, or if their efficiency at work is damaged. Where in such circumstances no complaint is made by the woman concerned, the result may be to strengthen the false stereotype that women are unreliable workers.

'Identifying the problem as one of sex discrimination ... helps to direct attention to the important point that sexual harassment is a barrier to the proper integration of women into the labour market, a barrier of the type which equal treatment laws should help to overcome.'

Sexual harassment at work: On the protection of the dignity of women and men at work, Luis Fina Sanglas, Director D.G. V., European Commission, EC Seminar on sexual harassment, 1991, The Hague, **the Netherlands.**

2. DEFINITION

2.1. Sexual harassment means unwanted conduct of a sexual nature, or other conduct based on sex affecting the dignity of women and men at work.[1] This can include unwelcome physical, verbal or non-verbal conduct.

There are two aspects of the definition of sexual harassment which have been adopted in European Community instruments which are especially striking.

The first is the focus in the definition upon how the conduct in question was regarded by the recipient rather than upon the motive or intention of the perpetrator in behaving that way. That the harasser was 'joking' or 'merely being friendly' may provide an explanation, but not an excuse.

The second aspect to be especially noted is the breadth of the definition. The European Commission Code recognizes that sexual harassment includes, but is not restricted to, sexual conduct. Sexual harassment often has nothing to do with an attempt to initiate sexual relations. It can be an exhibition of power or even hostility. The Code acknowledges this reality by including in the definition 'other conduct based on sex' affecting the dignity of women and men at work.

The following list of examples of what can be regarded as falling within the European Commission definition may be helpful.

Physical conduct of a sexual nature is commonly regarded as meaning unwanted physical contact ranging from unnecessary touching, patting or pinching or brushing against another employee's body to assault and coercing sexual intercourse. Much of this conduct, if it took place in the street between two persons, would amount to a criminal offence.

---

[1] Council Resolution on the protection of the dignity of women and men at work, (OJ C 157, 27.6.1990, p. 3, point 1).

Verbal conduct of a sexual nature may include unwelcome sexual advances, propositions or pressure for sexual activity; continued suggestions for social activity outside the workplace after it has been made clear that such suggestions are unwelcome; offensive flirtations; suggestive remarks, innuendoes or lewd comments. Such behaviour defines women's role as sexual objects rather than as work colleagues.

Non-verbal conduct of a sexual nature refers to the display of pornographic or sexually suggestive pictures, objects or written materials; leering, whistling, or making sexually suggestive gestures. This behaviour may make women feel uncomfortable or threatened and undermine the position of a woman who seeks to deal with her fellow employees with professional dignity.

Sex-based conduct refers to conduct that denigrates or ridicules or is intimidatory or physically abusive of an employee because of his or her sex, such as derogatory or degrading abuse or insults which are gender-related and offensive comments about appearance or dress. Such conduct can create an offensive working environment for the recipient.

2.2. Thus, a range of behaviour may be considered to constitute sexual harassment. It is unacceptable if such conduct is unwanted, unreasonable and offensive to the recipient; a person's rejection of or submission to such conduct on the part of employers or workers (including superiors or colleagues) is used explicitly or implicitly as a basis for a decision which affects that person's access to vocational training or to employment, continued employment, promotion, salary or any other employment decisions; and/or such conduct creates an intimidating, hostile or humiliating working environment for the recipient.[1]

The Code of Practice distinguishes between sexual harassment which damages the employee's working environment and sexual

---

[1] Council Resolution on the protection of the dignity of women and men at work (OJ C 157, 27.6.1990, p. 3, point 1).

harassment which, in addition, is used as the basis for employment decisions affecting the victim. The latter has been termed 'sexual blackmail' or 'quid pro quo' harassment, because sexual compliance is required in exchange for job advantages or the avoidance of disadvantages.

Sexual blackmail, by definition, involves an abuse of authority because only someone with supervisory or managerial authority has the power to threaten or take an employment decision affecting the person harassed. The key to establishing whether there has been harassment of this form is evidence of a link between rejection of the sexual advance and the detrimental treatment of the victim: for example, was the rejection of the advance a factor in a woman losing her job or promotion or in her being transferred?

Even where no tangible employment benefits are lost, it is well-documented that sexual harassment has adverse consequences for the victim's psychological, emotional and physical well-being. Sexual harassment can poison the working environment and the environment in which an employee must work can be viewed as a condition of her employment. Therefore, the European Community instruments also define sexual harassment as 'unwanted conduct of a sexual nature, or other conduct based on sex affecting the dignity of women and men at work' which 'creates an intimidating, hostile or humiliating working environment for the recipient'. Where such consequences can be shown, the women who have to work in such a sexually offensive working environment can be said to enjoy less favourable working conditions than their male colleagues.

'Principles for protection against sexual harassment at work

Sexual harassment at work is any conduct of a sexual nature unwanted by the recipient and which infringes her dignity as a person. It includes, for instance, physical contact and invasion of personal space, comments of a sexual nature, displaying pornographic images and making sexual propositions. Sexual harassment can be expressed verbally, in deeds, gestures or other sexually charged behaviour.

Sexual harassment is especially reprehensible when a power relationship is exploited, particularly where promises of professional advantages or threats of professional disadvantages are concerned.'

House Regulations No 1/92, Ministry of Women and Youth, **Germany.**

2.3. The essential characteristic of sexual harassment is that it is unwanted by the recipient, that it is for each individual to determine what behaviour is acceptable to them and what they regard as offensive. Sexual attention becomes sexual harassment if it is persisted in once it has been made clear that it is regarded by the recipient as offensive, although one incident of harassment may constitute sexual harassment if sufficiently serious. It is the unwanted nature of the conduct which distinguishes sexual harassment from friendly behaviour, which is welcome and mutual.

Romantic relationships are often formed at the place of work. But romance is consensual. This portion of the Code emphasizes that sexual harassment, by definition, is not 'romantic' or 'sexy' because it is imposed on the recipient. Indeed, behaviour which results in distress for the woman concerned suggests a dislike of women by the perpetrator. Even the gregarious and flirtatious man who gives his female colleagues a hug is showing arrogance and contempt for a woman's feelings if he persists in this behaviour after it has been made clear to him that it is unwelcome.

The Code stresses the important principle that it is for the individual woman to determine what offends her and what she welcomes or is prepared to accept. As in her life outside work, a woman at work must have the right to differentiate between the treatment she will accept from one man and from another. As the UK Employment Appeal Tribunal put it in the case of *Wileman* v *Minilec Engineering Ltd,* 'a person may be quite happy to accept the remarks of A or B in a sexual context, and be wholly upset by

24

similar remarks made by C'. By welcoming certain behaviour from one work colleague, a woman does not confer a licence upon all other colleagues to treat her in the same way.

By emphasizing that 'it is for each individual to determine what behaviour is acceptable to them and what they regard as offensive', the Code makes clear that the right to be treated with dignity is an individual right. In particular, it is not dependent upon the culture of the workplace or subject to the majority view of colleagues. That others acquiesce in a working environment polluted by sexual harassment does not deprive an individual of her or his right to object. Nor is it appropriate to permit different standards as between the office and the workshop. It is well documented that many women are reluctant to seek employment in certain traditionally male occupations precisely because they are made to feel uncomfortable by the harassment in the working environment.

The concept of 'harassment' may suggest repeated incidents. However, that does not permit a perpetrator to commit any act of harassment, so long as it is only done once. There are some forms of conduct which are sufficiently serious and obvious as to be almost inherently offensive. Physical violence or non-consensual touching of intimate body parts are examples of behaviour which it is reasonable to regard as sexual harassment the first time it occurs.

'Sexual harassment is unwanted attention of a sexual nature. Whether or not this sexually tainted attention is deliberate or unintended is of no importance. If the person who gets the attention is bothered by it, the behaviour is to be considered sexual harassment.

What is considered unwanted by one person is not necessarily a problem for another. Someone can accept the intimate behaviour of one person and consider the same behaviour by another person unwanted. It is always up to the recipient to judge whether or not something is unwanted.'

'Sexual harassment, it works better without it', Guidelines for employees, Postbank, **the Netherlands.**

3. THE LAW AND EMPLOYERS' RESPONSIBILITIES

3.1. **Conduct of a sexual nature or other conduct based on sex affecting the dignity of women and men at work may be contrary to the principle of equal treatment within the meaning of Articles 3, 4 and 5 of Council Directive 76/207/EEC of 9 February 1976 on the implementation of the principle of equal treatment for women and men as regards access to employment, vocational training and promotion and working conditions.[1] This principle means that there shall be no discrimination whatsoever on grounds of sex either directly or indirectly by reference in particular to marital or family status.**

This passage follows the language of the Council Resolution and Commission Recommendation. The fact that the Council Resolution and the Commission Recommendation say that sexual harassment '*may*, in certain circumstances, be contrary to the principle of equal treatment within the meaning of ... Directive 76/207/EEC' would not appear to be intended to detract from the generality of that principle. The use of the words 'may in certain circumstances' simply recognizes that there are certain factual situations which may possibly fall outside the scope of the prohibition on unequal treatment by employers : a situation where the employer neither knew, nor could have been expected to know, of the harassment, for example.

3.2. **In certain circumstances, and depending upon national law, sexual harassment may also be a criminal offence or may contravene other obligations imposed by the law, such as health and safety duties, or a duty, contractual or otherwise, to be a good employer. Since sexual harassment is a form of employee misconduct, employers have a responsibility to deal with it as they do with any other form of employee misconduct as well as to**

---

[1] OJ L 39, 14.2.1976, p. 40.

refrain from harassing employees themselves. Since sexual harassment is a risk to health and safety, employers have a responsibility to take steps to minimize the risk as they do with other hazards. Since sexual harassment often entails an abuse of power, employers may have responsibility for the misuse of the authority they delegate.

Where sexual harassment constitutes an actual physical assault or molestation, it is treated in all countries as a criminal offence. In some Member States, notably France and Germany, use of the penal code has been one of the principal legal remedies available for women sexually harassed at work. In France, sexual harassment by supervisors has been specifically addressed by an amendment to the penal code.

Most Member States impose a legal duty upon employers to provide a safe and healthy working environment. There is ample evidence that sexual harassment may result in an environment which is neither 'healthy' nor 'safe' for the victim(s) (and possibly her colleagues). However, at the time of writing, health and safety law remains a theoretical rather than a practical remedy for this problem in the Member States.

In most Member States, an employer has a duty not to undermine the employee's dignity or integrity as a worker. This may derive from express obligations in civil codes or labour codes or from implied or subsidiary contractual obligations. It is expressed in a variety of ways, including as a duty of mutual trust and confidence; obligations relating to physical, emotional and psychological working conditions; a duty to maintain physical and moral integrity; offences against the personality; and respect for the dignity of workers. In Spain, the obligation on an employer to ensure respect for a person's privacy is embodied in the Labour Code. In the Netherlands, at the time of writing, the government has announced its intention to extend the obligation of the employer under the health and safety law to cover a duty to combat and prevent sexual harassment. In Belgium, as noted below, labour legislation on working regulations has been amended to require employers to set out the measures to be taken to protect employees against sexual harassment at work.

There is now case-law in each of the Member States of the Community which has held that dismissal for refusing to submit to a sexual advance, or in retaliation for complaining about harassment, does not fall within the standard of fairness required whether that be expressed as 'reasonable in the circumstances', 'with just cause', 'socially warranted', etc.

An employer must ensure:

Respect for a person's privacy and dignity, including protection against verbal or physical insults of a sexual nature.'

Workers Charter, 5272 Act 3/1989 of 3 March 1989— s.4(2)(e), **Spain.**

'The employer shall:

(i) establish a good working environment and maintain it;

(ii) apply disciplinary sanctions against anyone who:
(a) through his behaviour provokes or creates conditions that have a demoralizing effect on the employee and on the women in particular (Art. 40(2) of the Legal Regulations for the individual worker's contract),
(b) violates the rights and the security of the company's employees (Art. 9(2)(b) of legal decision 64-A/89 of 27 February),
(c) uses physical violence within the company against employees of the company and/or utters terms of abuse or other insults which are punishable by law (Art. (9)(2)(i) of legal decision 64-A/89 of 27 February).'

'No sexual harassment at the workplace', Committee on Women's Conditions, **Portugal.**

'Article 1 — Employers who are required to draw up work regulations in accordance with Article 4 of the Act of 8 April 1965 on employment regulations, shall be obliged to state in those regulations, the measures laid down to protect employees against sexual harassment at work, in addition to the information set out in Article 6 of said Act.

These measures shall especially encompass a policy statement concerning sexual harassment at work, the designation of a confidential counsellor or service charged with the care, assistance and support of victims, the complaints-handling procedure and the disciplinary measures that may be taken.

Sexual harassment includes any form of verbal or physical conduct of a sexual nature, which the perpetrator knows, or should know, infringes upon the dignity of women and men at work.

Article 2 — In order to implement Article 11 and following of the Act establishing employment contracts of 8 April 1965, the employer shall be required, within three months after the announcement of this resolution, to submit to the works council a draft employment contract adapted in accordance with Article 1 or, if there is no works council, to bring this draft contract to the employees' notice by posting it.'

Royal Decree to protect workers against sexual harassment at work, 18 September 1992, Ministry of Employment and Labour, **Belgium.**

'Section 12

(1) The responsibilities of employees in managerial positions include combating the sexual harassment of employees and investigating cases of sexual harassment when they become known.

(2) Sexual harassment means, in particular, gratuitous bodily contact imposed on the recipient, unwelcome comments of a sexual nature, offensive comments, remarks or jokes about the appearance of an employee, displaying porno-graphic images at work and urging sexual contact.

(3) Sexual harassment is a breach of the employee's duty within the meaning of the definition in the regional disciplinary regulations.

(4) A recipient must not suffer disadvantages as a result of submitting a complaint.'

Regional Anti-discrimination Act (LADG, 31 December 1991), Federal State of Berlin, **Germany.**

'Article 222.33

The act of harassing others by means of orders, threats or force with the aim of obtaining favours of a sexual nature, by a person abusing the authority he derives from his office, shall be punishable by a year's imprisonment and a fine of FF 100 000.'

Penal code, 1992, **France.**

'The director admitted to a sexual interest in the complainant and to initiating, pursuing and fulfilling that interest. He claimed as a defence that all his actions were with the consent of the claimant.

In considering the question of consent, and in view of the worker's denial of consent, the Court must have regard to the director's dominant position in the employment relationship with all the power inherent in that position, the fact that he took advantage of the work-related arrangements in the hotel, to the fact that he did not have a social relationship with the worker outside of the workplace, and that he was aware of the personal vulnerability of the worker. In these circumstances, the Court does not accept the claim of consent.

A sexual relationship between consenting adults does not imply that the consent is unlimited as regards either time-scale or acts which may take place between the parties. Each party has the continuing right to place limitations on what acts may take place and when they may take place, and also a right to withdraw consent totally. These rights acquire the protection of the Employment Equality Act 1977, when the parties concerned are in a relevant employment situation. Consent may be varied at will and, provided the other party is made aware of the position, any act committed outside of the immediate consent is in breach of the 1977 Act.' (Compensation of IRL 9 000 awarded.)

A company v *A worker*, Labour Court, 29 June 1990, **Ireland.**

3.3. **This Code, however, focuses on sexual harassment as a problem of sex discrimination. Sexual harassment is sex discrimination because the gender of the recipient is the determining factor in**

who is harassed. Conduct of a sexual nature or other conduct based on sex affecting the dignity of women and men at work in some Member States already has been found to contravene national equal treatment laws and employers have a responsibility to seek to ensure that the work environment is free from such conduct.[1]

The concept of sexual harassment originated in a sex discrimination context in the United States. The governing principle in the case of harassment of a woman by a man is that the employee would not be harassed were she a man rather than a woman. Where men in the same situation are not harassed, the unequal treatment is on grounds of gender and thus discriminatory.

The same principle applies to harassment of a man by a woman, or indeed to cases of homosexual harassment. The principle that sexual harassment is sex discrimination, which contravenes national equal treatment laws, has been recognized by case-law in Denmark, Ireland and the United Kingdom at the time of writing.

The fact that a perpetrator may single out a particular woman for sexual harassment does not make the behaviour any less a sex discrimination issue. It is a fundamental principle of equal treatment law that a complainant does not have to prove discrimination against the whole group to which they belong; it is sufficient to show discrimination against the complainant because of her membership of the group (i.e. that she has been treated less favourably than a man has been, or would have been, treated).

> 'Although in some cases it will be obvious that there is a sex-related purpose in the mind of a person who indulges in unwanted and objectionable sexual overtures to a woman or exposes her to offensive sexual jokes or observations, that is

---

[1] Council Resolution on the protection of the dignity of women and men at work, 90/C 157/02, 27.6.90, s.2.3(a).

not this case. But it does not follow that because the campaign pursued against Mrs Porcelli as a whole had no sex-related motive or objective, the treatment of Mrs Porcelli by Coles, which was of the nature of "sexual harassment" is not to be regarded as having been "on the ground of her sex" within the meaning of s.1(1)(a) (of the British Sex Discrimination Act). In my opinion this particular part of the campaign was plainly adopted against Mrs Porcelli because she was a woman. It was a particular kind of weapon, based upon the sex of the victim which, as the Industrial Tribunal recognized, would not have been used against an equally disliked man.

... a material part of the campaign against Mrs Porcelli consisted of "sexual harassment", a particularly degrading and unacceptable form of treatment which it must be taken to have been the intention of Parliament to restrain.'

Strathclyde Regional Council v *Porcelli*, Scottish Court of Session, 1986, IRLR 134, **United Kingdom.**

'Freedom from sexual harassment is a condition of work which an employee of either sex is entitled to expect.' The Labour Court will 'treat any denial of that freedom as discrimination within the terms of s.3(4) of the Employment Equality Act.'

A worker v *A garage proprietor*, Labour Court, 1985, **Ireland.**

'After hearing the evidence, the court finds that the defendant's former foreman M. had made sexual approaches to the plaintiff during the plaintiff's employment by the defendant, but had been rejected, and that during a drive at the beginning of the month of December 1986, he once again made approaches to her, but had been vigorously rejected.

Immediately thereafter the plaintiff was relieved of all her duties by M., without any actual grounds for this being evident. When the plaintiff thereafter made a complaint to the other board members of the defendant, she was dismissed by M. Under these circumstances, the defendant is found to have violated paragraph 4 of the law (Danish Equal Treatment Act), and the plaintiff is considered to have rightfully claimed compensation, estimated at DKR 40 000.'

Supreme Court of Ostre Landsrets, *K* v *Danish Special Workers Union*, 8 September 1989, **Denmark.**

33

3.4. As sexual harassment is often a function of women's status in the employment hierarchy, policies to deal with sexual harassment will be most effective where they are linked to a broader policy to promote equal opportunities and to improve the position of women. Advice on steps which can be taken generally to implement an equal opportunities policy is set out in the Commission's Guide to positive action.[1]

Sexual harassment reflects general attitudes which perpetuate the view of women as sexual objects rather than equal members of the workforce. Sexual harassment policies will be more effective when linked with broader equal opportunities policies geared towards improving the overall position of women in the organisation. Research has shown that the likelihood of sexual harassment diminishes when the ratio of female to male employees is equal and when they are equally distributed over the various levels in the organizational hierarchy.

Conversely, policies to promote equal opportunities and improve the position of women are unlikely to be effective unless sexual harassment is addressed. In reality, sexual harassment is frequently more about power than about sex. It is often used as a weapon to 'keep women in their place'. That is why women in non-traditional women's jobs, such as those who have been the beneficiaries of positive action, are particularly liable to be harassed.

'Positive action aims to complement legislation on equal treatment and includes any measure contributing to the elimination of inequalities in practice.

---

[1] *Positive action: equal opportunities for women in employment — a guide*, OPE, 1988.

The setting-up of a positive action programme allows an organization to identify and eliminate any discrimination in its employment policies and practices, and to put right the effects of past discrimination.

Thus a positive action programme is a type of management approach which an employer can adopt with a view to achieving a more balanced representation of men and women throughout the organisation's work-force and thus a better use of available skills and talents.'

Positive action: equal opportunities for women in employment — a guide, Office for Official Publications of the European Communities, 1988.

'Women working in an environment where both sexes are equally represented display the lowest number of cases of sexual harassment at work (23.5%). Those who work in an environment where men are in a majority mention the highest number of cases (39.2%). We may conclude that men who work in an environment where women are in a minority are less aware of behaviour pertaining to sexual harassment. They think it is part of the work, while men who have as many male as female colleagues are much more aware of it.'

Sexual harassment at work: a study of the phenomenon in Athens, J. Manganara, Greek League for Women's Rights, **Greece** .

'Positive action for women

Koninklijke PTT Nederland NV (Royal Postal and Telecommunications Company in the Netherlands) pursues a positive action policy aimed at eliminating the disadvantaged position of women in relation to men within the company. The policy aims to achieve an equal representation of women at all job levels by improving the status of women within the company.

The PTT aims to remove the obstacles for women by means of the positive action agreements. One of the agreements concerns sexual harassment.'

'Working climate and unobjectionable conduct

The company takes measures to create and maintain a working climate conducive to the participation of women in the working process. By means of public relations and information, and through preventative as well as corrective measures, the company seeks to ensure a woman-friendly working environment and a good working atmosphere.

As sexual harassment is considered a form of behaviour harmful to employees and to the company, a committee of counsellors has been set up at head office with prevention as its major task. A person may also turn to the committee of counsellors for mediation when no solution can be found within the person's own division of the company.

The complaints procedure continues to be fully applicable in these situations.'

Company scheme, Koninklijke PTT Nederland NV, **the Netherlands**.

3.5. Similarly, a procedure to deal with complaints of sexual harassment should be regarded as only one component of a strategy to deal with the problem. The prime objective should be to change behaviour and attitudes, to seek to ensure the prevention of sexual harassment.

Effective procedures are essential, but they only address the harm after it has been inflicted. Much behaviour which is offensive may be a product of misunderstandings between women and men about what is unwelcome and what is acceptable. Training and communication strategies are needed to make both men and women aware of the issues surrounding sexual harassment and of the organization's policy to deal with it.

'The City of Amsterdam is striving for equal chances, rights and opportunities for all its employees. Sexual harassment hinders accomplishment of this goal and should therefore be prevented and combated.

(...)

At the same time we would like to take measures on three levels:
— prevention (public education, provision of information and training)
— counselling (of those who have been confronted with sexual harassment)
— combating harassment (complaints handling)

To some extent the preventive effect of public education and provision of information and training hinges, of course, on the other measures to be taken.

Information and publicity play a role in raising the consciousness of (male and female) personnel ... and are indispensable tools.

The possibilities are (in brief): presenting information on the issue in staff publications, special folders, theme-specific employee meetings, and courses for management and members as representative committees.'

Memorandum: From Sexual Harassment to Irreproachable Conduct. City of Amsterdam, **the Netherlands.**

4. COLLECTIVE BARGAINING

4.1. The majority of the recommendations contained in this Code are for action by employers, since employers have clear responsibilities to ensure the protection of the dignity of women and men at work.

Sexual harassment at work cannot be dismissed as a 'personal' dispute between employees. It is now acknowledged to be a problem for employers to address because it is the employer who has legal responsibility for the working environment in which harassment is permitted and it is the employer who has the power to take the measures necessary to change the workplace practice and culture so as to minimize the risk of sexual harassment.

> 'Unice agrees that sexual harassment at work must be condemned and prevented. Both employers and employees have the responsibility to create a climate at work which is free from unwanted conduct of a sexual nature.
>
> Because concrete measures in this field are best taken at the level of the firm, Unice approves the instrument chosen by the Commission, i.e. a Commission Recommendation and a Code of Practice. In Unice's opinion, it is important to state the objective, i.e. prevention of sexual harassment, and the Code of Practice is an example of how this could be done.'
>
> Comments on draft Commission Recommendation and Code of Practice, **Unice.**

4.2. Trade unions also have responsibilities to their members and they can and should play an important role in the prevention of sexual harassment in the workplace. It is recommended that the question of including appropriate clauses in agreements is examined in the context of the collective bargaining process, with the aim of achieving a work environment free from unwanted conduct of a sexual nature or other conduct based on sex, affecting the dignity of women and men at work and free from victimization of a

complainant or of a person wishing to give, or giving, evidence in the event of a complaint.

When the issue has been addressed in practice, preventing sexual harassment has usually proved to be an area for cooperation and consensus rather than a source of conflict between both sides of industry.

'The parties hereto ... recommend that the individual enterprise, through its personnel policies, seeks to ensure that the working environment is free from:

(a) unwanted conduct of a sexual nature or other conduct based on sex affecting the dignity of women and men at work,
(b) victimization of a complainant or of a person wishing to give or giving evidence in the event of a complaint.'

Collective agreement on equal treatment, Danish Employers' Confederation and Danish Confederation of Trade Unions, 2 July 1991, **Denmark.**

'Article 41. Infringements committed by workers:

...

Very serious infringements may be:

5. The lack of respect for a worker's privacy and proper consideration for his/her dignity, including verbal or physical offences of a sexual nature.

Article 42. Sanctions

Depending on the gravity of the offence, sanctions which may be applied shall be as laid down:

...

(C) Very serious offences:

(a) suspension of work and of wages for from 11 days up to two months;
(b) ban on entitlement to promotion for a period of two years or indefinitely;
(c) dismissal.

Where the scale of disciplinary measures is to be determined, the grade of responsibility and professional category of the offender, and repercussions of the occurrence on the undertaking and its workers shall be taken into account. As regards proceedings for offences, the provisions as laid down in Article 60.2. of the Workers' Charter shall apply.

...

Article 44. Abuse of authority

Where a worker believes that an abuse of authority by a superior has taken place, (s)he shall notify this through the workers' representative directly to the management.

After having received the complaint, the management shall proceed to investigate and determine with the shortest possible delay the relevant measures to be taken. Where sanctions may be imposed, they shall be in accordance with those determined in Article 42 of the agreement.

Workers shall enjoy basic rights in accordance with the definition and scope laid down in specific legislation on the subject, including the right of respect for his/her privacy and proper consideration for his/her dignity, including the protection against verbal or physical offences of a sexual nature. Any behaviour of the employer contrary to the respect for a worker's privacy and proper consideration for his/her dignity shall constitute an offence under this agreement.'

Collective agreement for travel agencies, **Spain.**

5. RECOMMENDATIONS TO EMPLOYERS

5.1. **The policies and procedures recommended below should be adopted, where appropriate, after consultation or negotiation with trade unions or employee representatives. Experience suggests that strategies to create and maintain a working environment in which the dignity of employees is respected are most likely to be effective where they are jointly agreed.**

In order to be effective, the separate recommendations made in the Code of Practice should not be viewed in isolation. Instead, each recommendation should be treated as part of an overall policy. For instance, merely appointing a confidential counsellor will not encourage those with complaints to come forward unless a clear policy is also introduced in which management explicitly states that they regard sexual harassment as a disciplinary offence.

Nor is it appropriate to adopt the recommendations of this Code without first ensuring that employees recognize its significance and without having given consideration to its practical implications for the particular organization concerned.

It is important that the policy not be one-sided, imposed from above. Employees will more readily allow superiors to appeal to their sense of responsibility if they and/or union representatives are involved in designing policies and procedures. This strengthens the base of support for policy in the organization.

> 'Do not "rush into" policy implementation in the wake of a crisis. A controlled exercise is usually much more successful.
>
> Do not attempt to introduce a sexual harassment policy into your workplace without making it part of a broader equal opportunities strategy.
>
> Do seek to involve any trade unions which may be active in your workplace. They can be a valuable source of training for

large parts of your work-force and may already have strict rules regarding sex and race harassment. A policy jointly developed and implemented by management and unions can be very successful.'

Introducing a sexual harassment policy in the workplace: an employers' guide, Women Against Sexual Harassment, **United Kingdom.**

5.2. It should be emphasized that a distinguishing characteristic of sexual harassment is that employees subjected to it often will be reluctant to complain. An absence of complaints about sexual harassment in a particular organization, therefore, does not necessarily mean an absence of sexual harassment. It may mean that the recipients of sexual harassment think that there is no point in complaining because nothing will be done about it, or because it will be trivialized or the complainant subjected to ridicule, or because they fear reprisals. Implementing the preventive and procedural recommendations outlined below should facilitate the creation of a climate at work in which such concerns have no place.

Even though research results imply that sexual harassment is a problem in every organization, many people do not think that sexual harassment occurs in their own workplace. A lack of formal complaints is often seen as evidence of that. However, if no specific policy exists in an organization, it is very likely that no complaints will be submitted.

Sexual harassment is a subject that people find difficult to discuss. The most common reactions to sexual harassment are feelings of confusion, powerlessness, humiliation, shock and fear. Most women do not consider themselves to be in a position to openly reject harassment. They worry about the consequences for their employment status, particularly if the perpetrator is a superior. Existing prejudices or the group atmosphere may also stop them from expressing their feelings, and they may prefer not to run the risk of receiving the blame or being accused by co-workers of spoiling the working atmosphere. Instead of public-ly raising the problem for discussion or filing a complaint, many women hope that the sexual harassment will just stop if they do not react, if they evade the perpetrator or if they put up with the situation.

A policy which focuses upon preventing and combating sexual harassment will break the silence and make the reporting of sexual harassment experiences easier.

'The development of a policy against sexual harassment is necessary even though there seem to be no explicit problems or complaints. There still is a strong taboo on sexual harass-ment. Research ... has shown, however, that even when there are no official complaints ... female employees suffer from sexual harassment at work. Therefore we can be sure it also occurs in our organization, causing problems for women, forcing them to resign, call in sick or ask for a transfer, especially since until now there has been no policy against sexual harassment.'

Policy memorandum on the legal position concerning sexual harassment at work — City of Dordrecht, **the Netherlands.**

5.A. Prevention

(i) Policy statements

5.A.1. **As a first step in showing senior management's concern and their commitment to dealing with the problem of sexual harassment, employers should issue a policy statement which expressly states that all employees have a right to be treated with dignity, that sexual harassment at work will not be permitted or condoned and that employees have a right to complain about it should it occur.**

A policy statement goes further than a general statement of the employer's intent 'to do something'. In a policy statement, the employer should address the employees directly and specify exactly what they can expect from the management and what the management expects from employees.

The object of the statement should be to convince everyone that there is no place for sexual harassment in the organization.

5.A.2. **It is recommended that the policy statement makes clear what is considered inappropriate behaviour at work, and explains that such behaviour, in certain circumstances, may be unlawful. It is advisable for the statement to set out a positive duty on managers and supervisors to implement the policy and to take corrective action to ensure compliance with it. It should also place a positive duty on all employees to comply with the policy and to ensure that their colleagues are treated with respect and dignity.**

Different people have different ideas about what constitutes sexual harassment. Without getting into detailed prescriptions for behaviour, it is advisable to include in the statement a description of what the management understands sexual harassment to be.

Preventing and combating sexual harassment requires joint effort on the part of both the employer and employees. The basic premise of the statement is that employers acknowledge their responsibility to prevent and combat sexual harassment on the one hand, and that employees understand their responsibility to treat co-workers with respect, on the other.

'Assurance to staff.

ESB wants to ensure that its work environment gives all employees the freedom to do their work without having to suffer sexual harassment from other staff members.

Sexual harassment is unlawful under the Employment Equality Act 1977. It can take many forms, e.g.:

(i)   unwanted verbal or physical advances,

(ii) words or actions of a sexual nature or with sexual undertones even if offence is not specifically intended,

(iii) display in the workplace of material of an explicitly sexual nature,

which are objectionable to the recipient, cause offence, discomfort or humiliation, or interfere with a person's ability to work.

It is the responsibility of management to ensure that the work environment of ESB is kept free from sexual harassment. It is important for everyone to understand what may constitute sexual harassment and regulate workplace conduct accordingly. Where there is a proper atmosphere or mutual respect, most difficulties which may arise should be capable of being sorted out amicably by the parties themselves taking a common-sense approach. However, a reliable procedure is necessary to deal fairly with allegations of sexual harassment when an aggrieved party considers it appropriate to make a formal complaint.

Sexual harassment can constitute grounds for disciplinary action and all employees should be aware of that.

> Because there can be sensitive and confidential aspects in such cases, the procedure is designed to safeguard the rights both of the aggrieved staff member and the person against whom the allegation is made. Most people will accept that it is better to sort out problems within the company if possible, but nothing in the procedure can overrule an individual's statutory right to process a complaint through the appropriate outside channels, i.e. the labour court or the civil courts.'
>
> Electricity Supply Board, **Ireland.**

5.A.3. **In addition, it is recommended that the statement explains the procedure which should be followed by employees subjected to sexual harassment at work in order to obtain assistance and to whom they should complain; that it contains an undertaking that allegations of sexual harassment will be dealt with seriously, expeditiously and confidentially; and that employees will be protected against victimization or retaliation for bringing a complaint of sexual harassment. It should also specify that appropriate disciplinary measures will be taken against employees found guilty of sexual harassment.**

Experience has proven that it is not easy to discuss sexual harassment openly, let alone to file a formal complaint. That is why it is best to mention explicitly in the statement that employees have the right to submit a complaint. However, the complainant then ceases to be anonymous and, consequently, runs the risk of being criticised by co-workers for having spoiled the atmosphere and relations at the workplace. For that reason, it is important that the employer states that action will be taken against any negative consequences of submitting a complaint.

Knowing the possibilities for assistance and the procedures which are available provides an incentive to come forward with the problem. In addition to information on the procedure, it is also crucial that management pledges to handle any complaints seriously, promptly and, as far as possible, confidentially.

Linking sanctions to sexual harassment has both a preventive and corrective effect. It makes sense to include this in the statement.

Potential perpetrators then know what they are getting themselves into, that transgressions will not be treated lightly, and that the issue is taken seriously.

(ii) Communicating the policy

A.4. Once the policy has been developed, it is important to ensure that it is communicated effectively to all employees, so that they are aware that they have a right to complain and to whom they should complain; that their complaint will be dealt with promptly and fairly; and so that employees are made aware of the likely consequences of engaging in sexual harassment. Such communication will highlight management's commitment to eliminating sexual harassment, thus enhancing a climate in which it will not occur.

As long as talking about sexual harassment is considered a taboo, little will change. That is why informing employees of the organization's policy is essential.

Employees can be informed about the sexual harassment policy in several different ways, such as:

(i)   through a special information brochure sent to employees when the policy is introduced;
(ii) by special information and discussion groups;
(iii) by placing the topic on the agenda of meetings of management, staff, work briefings or employee representatives;
(iv) by written information for new employees.

The most appropriate method will vary from organization to organization. It is advisable to use customary methods of providing information as much as possible.

If it can be anticipated that the topic will evoke a great deal of resistance, it may be helpful to make the information part of a subject that is less delicate, such as issues affecting the working

environment. Regular discussion of the subject of sexual harassment will diminish resistance and make it possible to talk about
the problem with less embarrassment.

'Communication

Specific reference to the Company's view on and procedure
for dealing with harassment matters to be included in Company Handbook, which employees should be made aware of.

Induction training to be used as a vehicle for ensuring all
future employees are communicated with.

Consider involvement of employee representatives in the
communication procedure.

Communication to be ongoing — notices, posters.

Definition of the minimum amount to be communicated, i.e. all
employees must be at least aware of the Company's statement on harassment, the basic definitions, the existence of the
complaints procedure, and the name and role of the counsellor.

Senior managers must be included in the communication
process, i.e. we must be aware of the dangers of focusing
downwards and never upwards.'

'Racial and sexual harassment guidelines', Fox's Biscuits,
United Kingdom.

(iii) Responsibility

**5.A.5. All employees have a responsibility to help to ensure a working
environment in which the dignity of employees is respected and
managers (including supervisors) have a particular duty to ensure
that sexual harassment does not occur in work areas for which
they are responsible. It is recommended that managers should**

explain the organization's policy to their staff and take steps positively to promote the policy. Managers should also be responsive and supportive to any member of staff who complains about sexual harassment; provide full and clear advice on the procedure to be adopted; maintain confidentiality in any cases of sexual harassment; and ensure that there is no further problem of sexual harassment or any victimization after a complaint has been resolved.

The attitude and conduct of managers serves as an example to other employees.

Those in managerial positions at all levels should see to it that the employees in their department are aware of the policy. They should also be expected to take action if sexual harassment occurs. That means that they must be capable of entering into discussions with both the complainant and the accused harasser.

Managers should also be able to talk about the topic in work, staff and departmental meetings and personally with individual employees where necessary, for example during performance appraisals.

Managers should keep their eyes and ears open for the various forms of sexual harassment and intervene if they observe them.

'The employer is responsible for creating a working climate in which people respect each other's dignity.

Management plays an essential role in carrying out the policy against sexual harassment: they are the first ones responsible for solving the problem when it occurs and for creating a working climate in which men and women respect each other's integrity. Experience shows that the attitude and reactions of management have a great influence on the behaviour of employees.

Management and personnel officers have a positive duty to give information on the problem and to set a standard for employees.'

51

Decree on Complaints Handling Procedure, Ministry of Finance for objectionable Conduct, Directorate General of Taxes, **the Netherlands.**

'Managers can do much to discourage sexual harassment, and have a contractual duty to prevent it taking place. In particular, managers should:

(i) be aware of the problems that sexual harassment can cause, and as part of their normal responsibilities be alert to the possibility that it may be happening;

(ii) ensure that the issue of sexual harassment is raised on central induction programmes, departmental induction programmes, and where necessary at section meetings, team briefings and works committees;

(iii) use their judgement in correcting standards of conduct or behaviour which could be seen as offensive, and to remind an employee(s) of the Council's policy and the department's code of disciplinary rules;

(iv) take prompt action to stop sexual harassment as soon as it is identified.'

Policy on sexual harassment, Reading Borough Council, **United Kingdom.**

'Often supervisors and managers notice some of the behaviour that later comes to be called harassment. It is useful for managers to increase their observation skills to spot possible problems. Some of the ways it may show itself are:

Informal Relations

Employees experiencing harassment often cite examples from their informal relations with other employees. The kind of behaviour you may observe and which may indicate a problem includes:

(i) when one or more employees are consistently left out of social invitations including lunch or if they always choose not to attend.

(ii) if there is a "joke" culture, do you have concerns about some of the comments? Do you think employees know when to stop? Is there undue pressure for employees to accept such banter?

(iii) where a particular ethos or culture has emerged, perhaps with some long-serving employees, is there likely to be pressure for any new employee to conform to this culture? Examples of workplace cultures might be where employees expect to become friends, where they are expected to talk about their personal lives, where there is joking or banter or where they are all reserved. While there is nothing wrong with some of these workplace cultures, it is important to realize that problems may emerge if an individual is forced to fit in with them.

(iv) does an individual appear to be ostracized by others?

Other Indicators

(i) Are other employees particularly critical of an individual or individuals? Are they reluctant to work cooperatively with them?

(ii) An employee has a high level of sickness absence whether medically certified or not, with stress-related illness.

(iii) Employees seem to lose motivation for their work, to be anxious, suddenly lacking in confidence or making a lot of mistakes.

Supervisors or managers may witness behaviour towards individuals, or generalized comments or actions not directed at anyone in particular which cause them concern. These may be tackled effectively by taking action quickly.'

'How to tackle harassment', London Borough of Ealing, **United Kingdom.**

(iv) Training

A.6. **An important means of ensuring that sexual harassment does not occur and that, if it does occur, the problem is resolved efficiently is through the provision of training for managers and supervisors. Such training should aim to identify the factors which contribute to a working environment free of sexual harassment and to familiar-**

ize participants with their responsibilities under the employer's policy and any problems they are likely to encounter.

Training is an effective method to prepare those in managerial positions for their task and will greatly enhance the results of other measures.

Many men (and sometimes women) find it hard to accept that their language, attitude or jokes may be viewed as sexual harassment. Managers must be prepared for this when policy measures take effect. They must possess the necessary skills to react appropriately if sexual harassment takes place in their presence or if they must confront those directly involved.

It is also crucial that they familiarize themselves with the reactions to and ramifications of sexual harassment and that they learn to recognize the signals that can be indications of sexual harassment.

'The Dortmund Social Research Centre conducts a practically oriented programme of change in order to contribute to the elimination of sexual harassment at work. This project seeks to provide support in dealing with the problem in the form of information, training and advice.

Developing, testing and finally organizing a training concept that can be used in educational tasks of union and company work are central to this plan. The objective is the prevention of sexual harassment in everyday work situations. The basic principle here is that positive processes of change cannot be achieved by action on the part of the women (recipients) alone and that this is not desirable either.

For this reason the training concept is not exclusively directed at this target group but rather involves the total social environment, i.e. colleagues and persons with responsibility within the company such as supervisors, members of worker or staff committees and instructors. These groups of people occupy central positions within the works communications system, and thus exercise an influence on the entire working atmosphere. Depending on individual attitudes and conduct they have a far-reaching effect on a working climate which, with regard to sexual harassment, can be either favourable or detrimental. In practice, the "multiplier effect" could be used as means for the prevention of a sexist working climate.

The training concept is developed on the basis of the following general objectives:

(i)   overcoming the separation and isolation of recipients and those with responsibility within the company;

(ii) providing background information on definitions of degree, consequences etc. of sexual harassment at work;

(iii) raising awareness as to discriminatory aspects in relations between the sexes;

(iv) strengthening individual possibilities of action;

(v)   developing possibilities to act within the structure of the company;

(vi) improving social skills in dealing with the issue at work;

(vii) providing information on legal aspects.'

'Well, just dress differently then', Training concept on sexual harassment at work, Social Research Office of the Dortmund State Institute, **Germany.**

A.7. In addition, those playing an official role in any formal complaints procedure in respect of sexual harassment should receive specialist training, such as that outlined above.

In addition to managers, other employees who have a specific responsibility in the implementation of policy must be trained to complete their task properly: personnel managers, company welfare workers and company doctors, confidential counsellors and staff charged with carrying out the complaints procedure.

Dealing with employees who are the victims of sexual harassment requires a keen insight into the nature of the problem and good conversational skills.

'Before the policy statement is published to staff generally, it is desirable that members of management and supervisory staff should be made aware of the terms of the policy statement and of the employer's commitment to the policy

contained in the statement. This should be accompanied by appropriate training and advice for management and supervisory staff in order to:
(i)   ensure consistent attitudes towards the problem;
(ii) ensure that complaints are dealt with through the grievance procedures to prevent the occurrence or recurrence of sexual harassment in the areas under their direct supervision or general control.'

'Personnel policies and procedures guidelines: Dealing with sexual harassment in the workplace', Federation of Irish Employers, **Ireland.**

'Training will be provided for managers, designated officers and members of any investigating, disciplinary, grievance or appeals panel.

No officer or Council member will play an official role in any formal procedure unless they have attended the training course.

The issue of sexual harassment will be included in all appropriate Council training courses e.g. induction, assertiveness training, equal opportunities.'

'Procedure for dealing with complaints of sexual harassment', Brighton Borough Council, **United Kingdom.**

5.A.8. **It is also good practice to include information as to the organization's policy on sexual harassment and procedures for dealing with it as part of appropriate induction and training programmes.**

Training can be particularly helpful in breaking through set patterns of conduct and interaction. Training can enable employees to distinguish between appropriate and inappropriate behaviour and it can provide them with a clear understanding of their rights and responsibilities.

Some employees may be reluctant to undergo specific training on sexual harassment. That is why sexual harassment should also be a set component of other training courses, such as:

(i)   management training,
(ii) courses for union-management committees or works councils,
(iii) social skills training for employees,
(iv) induction programmes for new employees.

'One should think of seminars for the women who are being harassed and other interested women in order to create a basis for assertive behaviour and a greater willingness to protest against and criticize the harasser openly.'

'Sexual harassment at work', Recommendations for action, Mr. Holzbecher, et al. Dortmund Institute for Social Research Ministry for Youth, Family, Women and Health, **Germany.**

'The employer can take the following initiatives:
(a) when recruiting personnel, point out to each new staff member that:
    (i) the company condemns and does not tolerate sexual harassment;
    (ii) in-house sanctions exist against it;
    (iii)such behaviour will be penalized;
(b) include in the contract of employment disciplinary measures against sexual harassment or other conduct based on sex.'

'Unwanted sexual behaviour: better to prevent than to cure', Ministry of Employment and Labour, Commission on Women and Labour, **Belgium.**

57

5.B. Procedures

3.1. **The development of clear and precise procedures to deal with sexual harassment once it has occurred is of great importance. The procedures should ensure the resolution of problems in an efficient and effective manner. Practical guidance for employees on how to deal with sexual harassment when it occurs and with its aftermath will make it more likely that it will be dealt with at an early stage. Such guidance should of course draw attention to an employee's legal rights and to any time limits within which they must be exercised.**

The complaints procedure is generally regarded as a crucial element for a successful policy against sexual harassment at work. In order to be effective, it should be made clear:

(i)   how and to whom the complaint should be filed;
(ii) what is expected both of the complainant and of the alleged harasser while the procedure is operating in respect of their rights and duties.

In drawing attention to an employee's legal rights, it should be made clear whether or not using the organization's internal procedure is mandatory and whether or not use of the internal procedure precludes the employee from taking legal action.

> 'If someone believes that you are harassing them, they may take informal action or formal action against you.
>
> Informal action
>
> If you are approached informally, the aim of the meeting is to resolve the situation and to avoid formal procedures, which might result in disciplinary action for yourself.
>
> If you are approached informally, look at the behaviour under question and see if you can modify it. If you believe that you are wrongly accused, and therefore are not prepared to change your behaviour, you may find that the individual complaining may want to take the matter further.

If you are approached by a manager or the Equal Opportunities Adviser informally about an alleged offence of personal harassment, you may need the support of a workplace colleague who knows you well, or a trade union representative. You are entitled to have them present, if you wish, at any informal meeting.

Formal Complaints

If you are approached as a part of a formal complaint against you, you are advised to seek the support of your trade union or a workplace colleague. You are entitled to have a representative or supporter with you at any formal meeting concerning the harassment investigation.

A formal complaint against you is serious. The Equal Opportunities Adviser investigating the complaint has to interview everyone concerned and to collect evidence (e.g. leaflets, pin-ups, statements) of the harassment. If the harassment complaint is upheld, disciplinary procedures will be instigated.

Information on this process is available from the Personnel Hand-book and Conditions of Service documents held by the staffing section of your department.

If you believe that the complaint against you is frivolous or malicious, your manager will investigate the matter and take any necessary action under the disciplinary procedure.'

'Personal harassment Code of Practice', Humberside County Council, **United Kingdom.**

(i) Resolving problems informally

5.B.2. Most recipients of harassment simply want the harassment to stop. Both informal and formal methods of resolving problems should be available.

It does not usually occur immediately to recipients of sexual harassment to file a formal complaint and to seek to have disciplinary action taken. They are inclined to think that having someone suspended or transferred is rather extreme and they tend to prefer an informal solution.

An informal settlement seeks to remedy the situation by directly confronting the harasser or by going through an intermediary (the boss, a co-worker, trade union representative or confidential counsellor).

A formal settlement means that a complaint is filed with the immediate supervisor or other person charged with the responsibility. The complaint is investigated and, if confirmed, sanctions may be imposed.

'How do you deal with sexual harassment?

In the first place — talk about it:

(i)   don't hide the fact that you are being harassed;
(ii)   it is not your fault;
(iii) describe the details in each case of harassment;
(iv)   check whether any change takes place in your work;
(v)   note whether the person harassing you changes his attitude towards you;
(vi)   find out if there is a purpose behind the harassment and if so what this purpose is;
(vii) find out whether other colleagues have similar problems, ask them for details;
(viii) discuss with these colleagues whether legal action should be taken;
(ix)   seek support from colleagues who have been victims — there may be witnesses in some cases;
(x)   regard the person harassing you as a problem for the working environment — not as your personal responsibility;
(xi)   speak openly about the person harassing you with your shop steward or a representative from the HK;
(xii) don't take on the fight single-handed, you are bound to lose.

'How to deal with sexual harassment?', HK (Clerical Workers Union), **Denmark.**

5.B.3. Employees should be advised that, if possible, they should attempt to resolve the problem informally in the first instance. In some cases, it may be possible and sufficient for the employee to explain clearly to the person engaging in the unwanted conduct that the behaviour in question is not welcome, that it offends them or makes them uncomfortable, and that it interferes with their work.

An informal approach may be adequate in instances involving a co-worker and when the sexual harassment is not very severe.

Men often do not realize that their behaviour might be objectionable and stop the behaviour as soon as they are confronted about it.

'The management wishes to encourage everybody troubled by sexual harassment to discuss their complaint at the earliest opportunity, preferably with the perpetrator, otherwise with a trusted colleague or other party.

The management realizes full well that those affected by sexual harassment may hesitate to defend themselves. The reasons may be shame, fear of trouble, fear of being exposed to badgering and ending up getting the blame oneself. The management are also acquainted with the popular argument that sexual harassment is usually invited by those who complain about it. We doubt whether this is often the case. We do know that superiors, or men in general, are more readily believed than women in discussions concerning, sexual harassment. We, the management, wish to avoid that trap.'

Policy statement by the management of Radio Nederland, **the Netherlands.**

5.B.4. In circumstances where it is too difficult or embarrassing for an individual to do this on their own behalf, an alternative approach would be to seek support from, or for an initial approach to be made by, a sympathetic friend or confidential counsellor.

Particularly when the woman involved is the only woman or one of the few women working in a department or organization with a male-dominated culture, it is commonly very difficult to confront the perpetrator. That is also the case when the harasser is a superior.

Sometimes mediation by a third party can be a solution. Whether that is an option or not depends on the position of the accused and the severity of the complaint. If the job levels of those involved differ too much, mediation will be more complicated. Mediation is also unlikely to be effective if the accused person denies having behaved objectionably or trivializes it.

'What is the challenge technique?

The challenge technique is an opportunity for someone who has experienced harassment to deal with the offending behaviour at their own pace and without the formal disciplinary procedure. It should be emphasized that the challenge technique is an option, it is not compulsory for a complainant to use it.

The challenge technique will be an option within existing "Council policy against sexual harassment — A Code of Practice" and any new harassment codes developed by the Council. It will enable the complainant in a harassment case to either directly challenge her harasser, accompanied by another person she will explain that she found certain behaviour offensive and that if that behaviour or similar behaviour is repeated she will make a formal complaint of harassment, or she can put her challenge in writing. She will then note down briefly her name and directorate and the directorate of the alleged harasser and write down the nature of the complaint, the date the challenge took place and the name of the person accompanying her. If she puts her challenge in writing she should keep a photocopy. She can either keep this herself or lodge it for safe keeping in a confidential file in the Central Equalities Team.

Why do we need this amendment to existing policy?

Many complainants in harassment cases do not want the formal management investigation with the resulting disciplinary or grievance hearing. It makes what is often an embarrassing and humiliating experience very public. Colleagues are not always supportive to the complainant and she may often experience hostility and even further harassment. Women are often not happy with the investigation and feel they have not been consulted but treated merely as a witness. Many people complaining of harassment do not want a big fuss, they just don't want the harassment to ever happen again.

The challenge technique will provide women with an opportunity to take control of their own harassment and to tell the harasser that the harassment must stop. Only the harasser and person accompanying her will be involved, unless the harassment continues.

Will the challenge technique become compulsory?

The challenge technique is an option but will never become a compulsory step in any harassment procedure. Some complainants in harassment cases may not feel able to confront their harasser or the complainant may want the harassment investigated by management. Obviously in cases of possible gross misconduct, the challenge technique is inappropriate. There should never be an expectation or an obligation to use the challenge technique. If a complainant wishes to use it, it is their choice.'

'The challenge technique', Eve Featherstone, Central Equalities Officer, Women, Haringey Council, **United Kingdom.**

'Those women who suffered sexual harassment said they felt very isolated and vulnerable at all levels, not knowing what to do and lacking information on the possible implications for their work that one or another mode of action might have. This demonstrates the urgent need for a specific function within companies, where women can obtain:
(i)   legal and financial advice,
(ii) psychological support,
(iii) confidentiality,
(iv) absence of pressure to report if not wanted by the woman concerned.'

'Sexual harassment at work', Ministry of Culture, Institute of Women's Affairs, **Spain.**

B.5. If the conduct continues or if it is not appropriate to resolve the problem informally, it should be raised through the formal complaints procedure.

The object of an informal settlement is to put a stop to the sexual harassment without negative consequences for the recipient. If the particular instance is an extremely severe form of sexual harassment (assault or rape), it should also be reported to the police.

(ii) Advice and assistance

3.6. It is recommended that employers should designate someone to provide advice and assistance to employees subjected to sexual harassment, where possible, with responsibilities to assist in the resolution of any problems, whether through informal or formal means. It may be helpful if the officer is designated with the agreement of the trade unions or employees, as this is likely to enhance their acceptability. Such officers could be selected from personnel departments or equal opportunities departments for example. In some organizations they are designated as "confidential counsellors" or "sympathetic friends". Often such a role may be provided by someone from the employee's trade union or by women's support groups.

It is important that the officer charged with providing support and advice does not take action without first receiving permission from the complainant.

The success of this function hinges on the confidence employees have in the person responsible. Confidence to a considerable extent depends on the accessibility of the person responsible.

In order to decide who should be given the task of providing advice and assistance, it is important to find out who — regardless of their position — is trusted by the (female) employees. The advantage of appointing an officer employed in the organization is that they are familiar with the job situation of those involved.

Since most complaints concern sexual harassment of women by men, women should be able to discuss the issue with a female officer. It is also important that the officer is available at a fixed time and location.

'The confidential counsellor allows the woman to tell her story. She offers help, gives information and advice. The confidential counsellor treats the complaints with strict confidentiality and only contacts a third party when the victim has given her permission to do so. The confidential counsellor gives assistance when the woman wants to file a formal complaint and takes care of the aftermath. In principle the confidential counsellor can mediate. Other than this the confidential counsellor:

(i)   registers and files the complaints;
(ii) gives information and produces publications which can contribute to awareness of the problem;
(iii) gives advice to the management with regard to policies against sexual harassment.'

Evaluation report — confidential counsellor, City Transportation, GVB Amsterdam, **the Netherlands.**

'The confidential counsellor has mediated in quite a number of cases. With regard to the interest of the plaintiff, this mediation is explicitly geared towards ending the sexual harassment. The confidential counsellor does not act in these situations as a referee but as the assistant to the victim.'

'Evaluation report of the sexual harassment confidential counsellor', University of Amsterdam, **the Netherlands.**

'Confidential advice

Group employers should designate an advisor(s) to whom those who feel they have been harassed, or who think they may have witnessed a case of harassment, may go for confidential advice. Advisors should be outside line management, have appropriate experience and understanding to counsel and advise individuals and ensure absolute confidentiality in the first instance. It is the duty of management to make sure that employees know the identity and location of their advisor.

At Sunbury Research Centre, Personnel has been designated to perform this advisory role. However, recognizing the sensitiveness of harassment situations it is emphasized that employees who feel they have experienced or witnessed harassment should go to whom they choose for help or advice. In the first instance this may be a work colleague, or to a line manager outside of their situation, or to a member of Personnel (not necessarily their own Personnel Officer), etc. In whichever way employees choose to deal with such situations, they are strongly encouraged to ensure it is reported to a representative of BP Research management so that appropriate action can be taken.'

'Confidential advice', Harassment policy, BP, **United Kingdom.**

3.7. Whatever the location of this responsibility in the organization, it is recommended that the designated officer receives appropriate training in the best means of resolving problems and in the details of the organization's policy and procedures, so that they can perform their role effectively. It is also important that they are given adequate resources to carry out their function, and protection against victimization for assisting any recipient of sexual harassment.

The officers responsible for providing advice and assistance can only perform this task satisfactorily if they can take action without the fear of negative consequences, even if the person accused of sexual harassment is their immediate supervisor or superior.

Therefore, it is advisable to provide that:

(i) the officer concerned must only be accountable to top management;
(ii) the support and counselling task must have no adverse consequences for their position as an employee;
(iii) nobody in the organization should be able to require the officer to release confidential information.

Preconditions for the task to be carried out correctly are that time, money and space be available. The officers must be able, for instance, to interrupt their regular work. Facilities such as a separate telephone line and a room suitable for confidential discussions will also improve the officer's accessibility and facilitate careful handling of the complaint.

'Working conditions:

(i) part of the working hours of the employee who is appointed as confidential counsellor is reserved for this duty or it is guaranteed that the confidential counsellor can leave her other job when required by her duties as confidential counsellor;

(ii) the confidential counsellor is directly responsible to the director;

(iii) the confidential counsellor will receive the necessary training;

(iv) the confidential counsellor will have a workplace that is properly equipped and a telephone line that cannot be interrupted by the operator;

(v) there will be ample publicity about the presence of the confidential counsellor, where she is located and when she can be reached.'

Memorandum: From sexual harassment to irreproachable conduct, City of Amsterdam, **the Netherlands.**

(iii) Complaints procedure

5.B.8. It is recommended that, where the complainant regards attempts at informal resolution as inappropriate, where informal attempts at resolution have been refused, or where the outcome has been unsatisfactory, a formal procedure for resolving the complaint should be provided. The procedure should give employees confidence that the organization will take allegations of sexual harassment seriously.

It is not easy to handle a complaint that could lead to disciplinary action if found legitimate. This may be a reason to first consider conducting a preliminary investigation in order to ascertain whether there are sufficient grounds for proceeding with a formal procedure.

'Because (name of employer) considers itself responsible for the social policies in its organization, it wishes to create a climate in which men and women respect each other's integrity. It therefore wishes to establish a complaints procedure which contains two phases:

1. Treatment of the complaint by a confidential counsellor.
2. Treatment of the complaint by a complaints commission.

(Name of company) has chosen a combination of confidential counsellor and complaints commission, because (name of company) hopes this may lead to an informal solution of most of the complaints, without the participation of the complaints commission being necessary.

(Name of company) thinks that a combination of a confidential counsellor and complaints commission will have a positive psycological effect.'

'Model for complaints procedure on sexual harassment', Algemene Werkgevers Vereniging (General Employers' Federation), **the Netherlands.**

3.9. **By its nature sexual harassment may make the normal channels of complaint difficult to use because of embarrassment, fears of not being taken seriously, fears of damage to reputation, fears of reprisal or the prospect of damaging the working environment. Therefore, a formal procedure should specify to whom the employee should bring a complaint, and it should also provide an alternative if in the particular circumstances the normal grievance procedure may not be suitable, for example because the accused harasser is the employee's line manager. It is also advisable to make provision for employees to bring a complaint in the first instance to someone of their own sex, should they so choose.**

According to most complaints procedures, the complaint must first be reported to the immediate supervisor. This rule cannot be followed if that person is the one who is accused of sexual harassment. Consequently, the procedure should also offer the option to bypass the immediate supervisor. Another way in which this can be done is by forming a special complaints committee to deal with allegations of sexual harassment by investigating whether a complaint is well founded and advising management on action to be taken.

The involvement of a special committee increases confidence that complaints will be handled objectively. Another advantage is that expertise is gained and complaints are handled with some uniformity. If individual supervisors are entrusted with the responsibility, there is a likelihood that important differences in approach will arise. Special committees should preferably comprise employee and employer representatives and consist of both women and men.

It is also important that the complaints procedure should be available not only to permanent employees, but also temporary workers, trainees or stand-by workers, since it is precisely these categories that are more likely to be confronted with sexual harassment.

'According to the Board of the Foundation of Labour, the special nature of complaints of sexual harassment makes it necessary, when using a general complaints procedure, to pay attention to the following points and, if necessary, to adjust any existing procedure:

(a) "Regular" complaints procedures are usually based on the principle that a complaint related to the work situation must initially be filed with the immediate superior. However, such a procedure is not suitable for a woman employee who is harassed by her superior or any other highly placed employee. It might be considered that, in that case, the complaint should be filed directly with the management. In view of this specific issue, the establishment of a special committee to handle complaints of sexual harassment may also be considered.

...

(e) Complaints are not always filed against people who are active in the same organization or who work for the same employer: employees may also be harassed by clients, suppliers or anyone else with whom the organization maintains relations; and more and more often, situations occur in which people employed by different employers work on the same shop-floor. It is also important to pay attention to such situations when establishing procedures.'

'Recommendation in respect of preventing and combating sexual harassment at work', Foundation of Labour, **the Netherlands.**

.10. It is good practice for employers to monitor and review complaints of sexual harassment and how they have been resolved, in order to ensure that their procedures are working effectively.

'In the Foundation's Recommendation respecting the right to complain, one of the issues pointed out is that in complaints procedures a provision shall be included stating that neither the employee filing a complaint nor the officer who deals with the complaint shall suffer negative consequences in respect of his or her position as an employee as a result of the complaint.

In cases of complaints of sexual harassment, this kind of protection is highly important. Research shows that filing a complaint of sexual harassment can have an adverse effect: even with a good complaints procedure and even if the complaint of the woman is upheld, she can still suffer greatly for it. Consequently, it may be useful for a member of the sexual harassment complaints committee or someone else in the organization to maintain contact with the woman complainant for some time after the complaint has been resolved.'

'Recommendation in respect of preventing and combating sexual harassment at work', Foundation of Labour, **the Netherlands.**

71

(iv) Investigations

5.B.11. **It is important to ensure that internal investigations of any complaints are handled with sensitivity and with due respect for the rights of both the complainant and the alleged harasser. The investigation should be seen to be independent and objective. Those carrying out the investigation should not be connected with the allegation in any way, and every effort should be made to resolve complaints speedily — grievances should be handled promptly and the procedure should set a time-limit within which complaints will be processed, with due regard for any time-limits set by national legislation for initiating a complaint through the legal system.**

The principle that both sides of the argument must be heard is fundamental to an investigation of a complaint.

It generally takes a few weeks to handle a complaint, which is a difficult time for all concerned. As soon as a complaint is filed, it may be necessary to take interim measures, for example if the complainant and the accused have to work together. In such a situation, a temporary reallocation of tasks can be a temporary solution.

It is advisable to draw up a written report of the evidence which has been given, and that each party is given the report of their evidence and confirms that it is accurate.

To enhance confidence in the objectivity of the proceedings, an organization may choose to involve an outside expert, such as a lawyer or labour inspector.

Very often, there are no witnesses to alleged acts of sexual harassment. This should not be regarded in itself as sufficient grounds for rejecting a complaint. In such a case, the investigation must proceed on the basis of whether the complaint is to be upheld according to the balance of such evidence as is available. This often involves an assessment of whether a complaint is plausible: for instance, whether the complainant discussed the harassment with her doctor, family, co-workers or friends, or whether her behaviour or demeanour changed after the alleged incident.

To facilitate correct handling, it is important to firmly establish the time period within which:

(i) the complainant is to receive a written confirmation of the complaint filed;

(ii) the investigation must be completed;

(iii) the complainant will be informed of the decision on the complaint and any further measures which will be taken.

'Procedure for setting up an investigation into sexual harassment at work.

Article 1. A staff member who is a recipient of unwanted sexual harassment at work can request a committee which has been set up for that purpose to open an investigation into the case.

Article 2. This request should be submitted to the 11th directorate, department of emancipation policy, whether by a confidential counsellor designated by that department or directly by the recipient.

Article 3. The investigation committee is charged with advising the recipient, the head of the department or the City Council on measures to be taken against a person accused of sexual harassment.

Article 4. This investigation committee comprises the following:

(i) chairperson: the inspector-general;

(ii) permanent members: a staff member of the 11th directorate charged with implementing the emancipation policy and a psychological counsellor;

(iii) additional members: may be the head of the department concerned, the confidential counsellor of the department concerned;

(iv) secretary: a staff member of the 11th directorate/emancipation policy department.

Article 5. The committee shall treat the complaint confidentially. It shall read the documents in the file, hear the witnesses it considers relevant, confer, and give its advice in case of a majority vote.

Article 6. The chairperson and the members are entitled to cast a conference vote during meetings, the secretary is not.

Article 7. The secretary shall prepare a report on the session. This report shall be signed by the chairperson, the permanent members present and the secretary.

Article 8. According to the case, the advice shall be made known to the recipient, head of the department or City Council.

Article 9. The persons called to attend the committee session shall be provided with the requisite departmental facilities to fulfil their obligations in this matter.'

City Council Ruling of 11 February 1991 (D11 or A09), City of Antwerp, **Belgium.**

'The complainant will be kept informed of progress during investigation. The facts of the allegation will be checked as discreetly as possible and an effort will be made to establish if any other staff have experienced similar problems with the alleged harasser.'

A model sexual harassment policy, Employment Equality Agency, **Ireland.**

5.B.12. **It is recommended as good practice that both the complainant and the alleged harasser should have the right to be accompanied and/or represented, perhaps by a representative of their trade union or a friend or colleague; that the alleged harasser must be given full details of the nature of the complaint and the opportunity to respond; and that strict confidentiality should be maintained throughout any investigation into an allegation. Where it is necessary to interview witnesses, the importance of confidentiality should be emphasized.**

To prevent rumours and backbiting from impeding the ongoing investigation, confidentiality is important, not only for the sake of the complainant and accused, but also for any witnesses or those conducting the investigation.

13. **It must be recognized that recounting the experience of sexual harassment is difficult and can damage the employee's dignity. Therefore, a complainant should not be required to repeatedly recount the events complained of where this is unnecessary.**

If the complainant does not want to face a direct confrontation with the accused, this request should be respected.

The complainant may decide during the procedure to withdraw the complaint, perhaps because the investigation evokes too much emotion or because of the consequences that the investigation will have for the accused.

In principle, the complaints procedure should stop as soon as the complainant indicates that she wants to withdraw. However, there may be exceptional cases where continuing the procedure is more important than respecting the complainant's wishes, such as if there is strong evidence that failing to take remedial steps will result in new complaints from other employees.

'The "harasser" may be disciplined by the employer either as a result of a grievance pursued by the "victim" or one initiated by management. Although at this stage the "victim" is only a witness there is still a need for representation. In such cases the woman's character, background, clothing, and so on may be called into question, something that can be a very traumatic experience. It is essential that the disciplinary procedure or the sexual harassment policy acknowledges this point and allows for the woman to be represented by the union.'

Dealing with sexual harassment, National and Local Government Officers Association, **United Kingdom** .

5.B.14. The investigation should focus on the facts of the complaint and it is advisable for the employer to keep a complete record of all meetings and investigations.

The only conduct of the complainant which is relevant to an investigation is conduct relating to the relationship between the complainant and the alleged harasser. An inquiry into a complainant's relations with other workers or private life not only is not relevant, but if it is permitted it will deter other complainants from coming forward.

(v) Disciplinary offence

5.B.15. It is recommended that violations of the organization's policy protecting the dignity of employees at work should be treated as a disciplinary offence; and the disciplinary rules should make clear what is regarded as inappropriate behaviour at work. It is also good practice to ensure that the range of penalties to which offenders will be liable for violating the rule is clearly stated and also to make it clear that it will be considered a disciplinary offence to victimize or retaliate against an employee for bringing a complaint of sexual harassment in good faith.

Treating sexual harassment as a disciplinary offence has a substantial preventative effect. Although all forms of sexual harassment are harmful to those affected, a distinction can be made between severe and less severe forms. Measures should correspond to and depend upon the severity of the sexual harassment.

Other factors should play a role in determining appropriate measures, such as whether the harassment involved an abuse of authority and the options for transfer in an organization. The key consideration, however, should be that the complainant should be able to work in a safe environment.

'Disciplinary punishments which primarily apply to sexual harassment are:

(i)   a written reprimand,
(ii) suspension, with or without wages,
(iii) dismissal.

The disciplinary punishment selected depends on the seriousness of the offence and the extent to which the offender (and sometimes also the plaintiff) can be blamed for this behaviour.

A very important aspect is the extent to which the offender occupies a position of power over the plaintiff. The selection of punishment will be influenced by the way in which the persons involved are still able to function at work after the offence. If required, a reprimand or suspension may be combined with a transfer, if this is necessary in the company's interest.'

Policy memorandum on the legal position concerning sexual harassment at work', City of Dordrecht, **the Netherlands.**

'Immediate dismissal by the employer is possible when the employee is found guilty of unreasonable or immoral behaviour or molesting (of any sort) at work.'

Collective Agreement between the Monopol-Scholer Group and the OGB-L,LCGB, FEP-FIT, **Luxembourg.**

16. Where a complaint is upheld and it is determined that it is necessary to relocate or transfer one party, consideration should be given, wherever practicable, to allowing the complainant to choose whether he or she wishes to remain in their post or be transferred to another location. No element of penalty should be seen to attach to a complainant whose complaint is upheld and in addition, where a complaint is upheld, the employer should monitor the situation to ensure that the harassment has stopped.

'If the Chief Officer is satisfied that sexual harassment has taken place, action will be taken in accordance with the agreed disciplinary procedure.

Where such action necessitates the transfer of one party from the section/department either on a temporary or permanent basis, it will be the harasser who is moved, not the complainant.'

'Procedure for dealing with complaints of sexual harassment', Derbyshire County Council, **United Kingdom.**

5.B.17. Even where a complaint is not upheld, for example because the evidence is regarded as inconclusive, consideration should be given to transferring or rescheduling the work of one of the employees concerned rather than requiring them to continue to work together against the wishes of either party.

When a complaint is not upheld, it is important that the complainant is not victimized for having brought the complaint, provided the accusation was made in good faith. If it is found that the complaint was brought maliciously, disciplinary proceedings against the complainant may be considered appropriate.

It is also important for management to take reasonable steps to ensure that the reputation of the alleged harasser is restored and that his career does not suffer by reason of the complaint having been brought against him. This may necessitate some public statement by the employer in respect of the incident.

Marks, M. *O glücklick, wer noch hoffen kann....*

6. RECOMMENDATIONS TO TRADE UNIONS

6.1. **Sexual harassment is a trade union issue as well as an issue for employers. It is recommended as good practice that trade unions should formulate and issue clear policy statements on sexual harassment and take steps to raise awareness of the problem of sexual harassment in the workplace, in order to help create a climate in which it is neither condoned nor ignored. For example, trade unions could aim to give all officers and representatives training on equality issues, including dealing with sexual harassment and include such information in union-sponsored or approved training courses, as well as information on the union's policy. Trade unions should consider declaring that sexual harassment is inappropriate behaviour and educating members and officials about its consequences is recommended as good practice.**

Trade union members can be the victims of sexual harassment and may lose their job as a result or have to work in the offensive environment which sexual harassment creates. Trade union members can also be the harassers. Therefore, there has been growing recognition by trade unions throughout the European Community that sexual harassment is a legitimate trade union issue.

Trade unions in most Member States continue to play a major role in raising awareness of the problem of sexual harassment by informing their members and officials through discussions, publications, posters and other means.

'The 13th Federal Conference of the DGB strongly opposes any form of sexual harassment: that means any sexual approaches either verbal or non-verbal, expressions of a sexual nature or discriminating remarks, which cause the recipient to feel threatened, humiliated, bothered or harassed.

The 13th Federal Conference of the DGB considers it necessary that the problem of sexual harassment should be the subject of an open discussion and reaffirms that dealing with the problem of sexual harassment is an integral part of the union's representation role.'

Decision by the 13th Federal Conference of the DGB, 1986, **Germany.**

'Title 5 — On discipline

Article 36 — Disciplinary sanctions

Any CGIL member whose behaviour is contrary to the principles of democracy and of the guarantee of other members' rights, which proves damaging to the trade union organization and which represents a violation of the principles and regulations of the Articles of Association, shall be subject to disciplinary sanctions.

The applicable sanctions shall be as follows, in order of severity:

(a) written reprimand;
(b) suspension from exercising membership rights and the resulting removal from any trade union office held for a period of one to 12 months;
(c) expulsion from the organization.

These sanctions shall be applied, taking into account the type and severity of the violation, for:

...

(b) sexual harassment and intimidation.'

Statutes of the CGIL, **Italy.**

'Sexual harassment of one NCU member by another (others) is not only unlawful under the 1975 Sex Discrimination Act, it also conflicts with Rule 3 (iv) of the Union which defines one of the objects of the NCU as "to oppose any force in society which seeks to foster division based on race, creed, religion, sex or sexual orientation". Sexual harassment is unwanted and unhealthy for the victim and divisive for the Union.'

'Code of Practice for dealing with complaints of sexual harassment within the NCU', National Communications Union, **United Kingdom.**

5.2. Trade unions should also raise the issue of sexual harassment with employers and encourage the adoption of adequate policies and procedures to protect the dignity of women and men at work in the organization. It is advisable for trade unions to inform members of their right not to be sexually harassed at work and provide members with clear guidance as to what to do if they are sexually harassed, including guidance on any relevant legal rights.

Trade unions should introduce the issue of sexual harassment in negotiations on collective agreements. They can promote this process by drafting a model agreement containing the most significant elements of a policy aimed at preventing and combating sexual harassment.

The basis for a collective agreement should be that both parties acknowledge that every worker has the right to have their dignity and human integrity respected. In their conduct with and towards each other, the employer and employees should mutually respect this right. Both parties should agree to make an active contribution, each in an appropriate way and with the proper means, towards preventing and combating sexual harassment at work.

Trade union officials should be asked to report back on the success they have achieved in negotiating collective agreements on sexual harassment.

The ETUC is putting forward four main strategies (...).

(i) A strategy for collective bargaining and collective agreements.

(ii) A strategy aimed at improving health and safety at work.

(iii) A strategy aimed at trade union organizations.

(iv) A strategy on recourse to legislation.'

Resolution on protection of the dignity of women and men at work — **ETUC Executive Committee** 5 and 6 March 1992.

'Internal measures:

(i) Distribution

Distribution of this document throughout the entire union structure, as a source of information and advice for all members.

(ii) Training

Proceeding from the principle that sexual harassment issues must be discussed openly by union members of both sexes, we propose organising mixed-gender courses or seminars at the leadership level as well as at the representative and committee level.

(iii) Investigation

... We suggest conducting surveys ... for the purpose of probing the extent to which sexual harassment problems are recognized in union circles and ascertaining how receptive trade union leaders are with respect to this issue.

(iv) Legal Advice

(v) Disciplinary measures

... members who are guilty of such activities will be subjected to disciplinary measures to be determined by the authorized bodies, in accordance with the procedure detailed in Article 10 of the Confederation Statutes.

External measures:

(i) Collective Labour Agreement negotiations:

Demand that clauses be adopted in the CLAs that firmly establish avenues for reporting sexual harassment and that state that this type of conduct is punishable.

(ii) Labour Inspectorates

Request labour inspectorates to create special vigilance campaigns against sexual harassment.'

'Trade Unions against sexual harassment at work', Women's secretariat CC.OO **Spain.**

5.3. Where complaints arise, it is important for trade unions to treat them seriously and sympathetically and ensure that the complainant has the opportunity of representation if a complaint is to be pursued. It is important to create an environment in which members feel able to raise such complaints knowing that they will receive a sympathetic and supportive response from local union representatives. Trade unions could consider designating specially trained officials to advise and counsel members with complaints of sexual harassment and act on their behalf if required. This will provide a focal point for support. It is also a good idea to ensure that there are sufficient female representatives to support women subjected to sexual harassment.

In dealing with an individual complaint of sexual harassment, the trade union official should discuss with the complainant what action she wishes to be taken and what action may be available. The official should ensure that the complainant is informed of any rights she has under the workplace complaints or grievance procedure.

Where a complaint arises, it may be appropriate for the union to investigate whether other workers have had similar problems with the alleged harasser.

Trade union officials commonly are men. This poses the same difficulty for the union as employers face in designing a complaints procedure: women who have been sexually harassed will normally prefer to speak about it in the first instance to another woman. One way in which trade unions can assist women in this respect is by creating a network of women members on a local, regional or national basis, to be available to advise members who have been subjected to sexual harassment.

As noted in the Code, it can also be helpful for a union to designate specially trained officials to act on behalf of victims of sexual harassment for the purpose of a complaints procedure.

'Title 1 — Founding principles

Article 2 — Basic principles

The CGIL shall safeguard, following the most appropriate methods and procedures, the right of all workers to fair and impartial relationships, especially with reference to possible sexual harassment and intimidation at the workplace.

Article 15 — Women's co-ordinating groups

...

The coordinating groups undertake to promote and achieve the active participation of all CGIL women in the groups' development and initiatives, taking the workplace as a starting point, and, in any case, to stress the importance of the groups' presence and of their role in the organization. The coordinating groups shall represent the CGIL in legal proceedings concerning sexual harassment and intimidation instituted by the trade union.'

Statutes of the CGIL, **Italy.**

6.4. It is recommended too, where the trade union is representing both the complainant and the alleged harasser for the purpose of the complaints procedure, that it is made clear that the union is not condoning offensive behaviour by providing representation. In any event, the same official should not represent both parties.

Unions should consider issuing a separate statement that sexual harassment of a union member by a union member is considered objectionable conduct.

When confronted with such a situation, the union is placed in a difficult position. The union may consider it appropriate to conciliate between the parties so as to put a stop to the offensive behaviour as quickly as possible. In principle, both the complainant and accused are entitled to the support and representation of the union.

Where separate union officials represent the complainant and the alleged harasser, it is important that the union ensure that the complainant is represented by an officer of at least the same rank as the officer representing the alleged harasser.

Trade unions should apply disciplinary measures to union officials who, by sexually harassing a member, have abused their position of trust and power.

Where formal disciplinary procedures are taken against a union member who has admitted harassing or who has been found to have harassed another union member, unions may wish to consider whether their representation of the member accused should be limited to ensuring that the hearing is conducted fairly.

> 'As a Ucatt official, either lay or full-time, your priority is to assist and represent the victim of sexual harassment. Often the only "evidence" will be one member's word against another. As with all grievances, you will have to make your mind up on each individual case. But if there is reasonable doubt, your job is to represent the victim.'
>
> Blueprint for equality, Ucatt, **United Kingdom.**

5.5. It is good practice to advise members that keeping a record of incidents by the harassed worker will assist in bringing any formal or informal action to a more effective conclusion; and that the union wishes to be informed of any incident of sexual harassment and that such information will be kept confidential. It is also good practice for the union to monitor and review the union's record in responding to complaints and in representing alleged harassers and the harassed, in order to ensure its responses are effective.

Trade unions should attempt to ensure that the employer takes prompt and appropriate remedial action in respect of complaints of sexual harassment brought by a member of the union.

If the response of the employer is not satisfactory, the union should consider supporting the complainant in an appropriate legal action. The union may also wish to consider referring the issue to a statutory advisory or enforcement agency, where this is available.

It is important for the union to monitor not just the result of complaints, but also to ensure that the complainant has not been victimized, either by co-workers or by management.

'Protecting personal dignity at the workplace

With reference to the initiatives under study within the EEC, in compliance with the resolution of the Council of the European Communities of 29 May 1990 on the promotion of campaigns and initiatives aimed at protecting the personal dignity of men and women in their working environment, as well as with reference to the establishment, in correspondence with the criteria to be defined at Community level and adopted in national legislation, of possible steps destined to combat any kind of objectionable conduct of a sexual nature which may infringe upon the personal dignity of men and women at work, the commission mentioned under Article 3 shall act as a watchdog, collecting data, information and regulations concerning the legal and normative developments in the field, which are to be brought to the knowledge of the contracting parties.'

Collective agreement, Telesoft/Intersind-Filpt-Silte-Uilte, **Italy.**

7. EMPLOYEES' RESPONSIBILITIES

7.1. **Employees have a clear role to play in helping to create a climate at work in which sexual harassment is unacceptable. They can contribute to preventing sexual harassment through an awareness and sensitivity towards the issue and by ensuring that standards of conduct for themselves and for colleagues do not cause offence.**

Sexual harassment is not merely a 'management problem' and still less a 'women's problem'. All employees have responsibilities as well as rights in respect of the working environment which is created. Sexual harassment, particularly in its less severe forms, can be part of the normal code of behaviour in a workplace. To change this may require each employee to question his own attitudes and conduct as well as that of his colleagues.

7.2. **Employees can do much to discourage sexual harassment by making it clear that they find such behaviour unacceptable and by supporting colleagues who suffer such treatment and are considering making a complaint.**

A major reason why few sexual harassment complaints get reported is that the person involved is afraid of co-workers' reactions. They do not want to run the risk of being accused by them of spoiling the work climate. Neither do they want to be told that they provoked the harassment themselves or that they cannot take a joke. When employees show through their words and actions that they find sexual harassment unacceptable, this will provide substantial support to those who are harassed and will ease filing a complaint.

'It is not easy to talk about sexual harassment. Even when we see it happen it is difficult to say something about it. If we want to prevent sexual harassment we must do something against it, for example, supporting the person who is being harassed. We can stop pretending that we didn't notice anything. We can show our disapproval and criticize the behaviour. Sexual harassment should not be part of the work.'

'Sexual harassment, it works better without it', guidelines for employees, Postbank, **the Netherlands.**

7.3. Employees who are themselves recipients of harassment should, where practicable, tell the harasser that the behaviour is unwanted and unacceptable. Once the offender understands clearly that the behaviour is unwelcome, this may be enough to put an end to it. If the behaviour is persisted in, employees should inform management and/or their employee representative through the appropriate channels and request assistance in stopping the harassment, whether through informal or formal means.

When telling the harasser that the behaviour is unwanted, if the employee does not want to confront the harasser alone, she may want to ask a co-worker or a friend to be present. An alternative to confronting the harasser in person is to put the complaint in writing, keeping a copy.

If the harassment continues, however, the employee should, if possible, seek advice on what to do next.

It is important for an employee subjected to sexual harassment to keep a record of the incidents so as to be able to recall exactly what has happened.

'If you feel that you are being harassed there are a number of steps you can take to deal with it. You have the right not to be harassed and you should not feel or be made to feel guilty or embarrassed about exercising your rights.

Make it clear to the harasser that his behaviour is unwelcome and ask him to stop.

If he does not stop the behaviour, make notes of the incidents and dates and report it immediately:

(i) to your union representative and employer, or if you have no union representative, report it to the appropriate management official or,

(ii) if the harasser is the union representative or appropriate management official, report the behaviour to a higher official or,

(iii) if none of these alternatives are available or if your employer is the harasser, report the matter to the Equal Opportunities Commission for Northern Ireland.'

'Sexual harassment is no laughing matter', Equal Opportunities Commission for Northern Ireland, **United Kingdom.**

ANNEX

COMMISSION RECOMMENDATION

of 27 November 1991 on the protection of the dignity of women and men at work (92/131/EEC)

THE COMMISSION OF THE EUROPEAN COMMUNITIES,

Having regard to the Treaty establishing the European Economic Community, and in particular the second indent of Article 155 thereof,

Whereas unwanted conduct of a sexual nature, or other conduct based on sex affecting the dignity of women and men at work, including the conduct of superiors and colleagues, is unacceptable and may, in certain circumstances, be contrary to the principle of equal treatment within the meaning of Articles 3, 4 and 5 of Council Directive 76/207/EEC of 9 February 1976 on the implementation of the principle of equal treatment for men and women as regards access to employment, vocational training and promotion, and working conditions,[1] a view supported by case-law in some Member States;

Whereas, in accordance with the Council recommendation of 13 December 1984 on the promotion of positive action for women,[2] many Member States have carried out a variety of positive action measures and actions having a bearing *inter alia*, on respect for the dignity of women at the workplace;

Whereas the European Parliament, in its resolution of 11 June 1986 on violence against women,[3] has called upon national

---

[1] OJ I 39, 14.12.1976, p. 40.

[2] OJ I 131, 19.12.1984, p. 34.

[3] OJ C 176, 14.7.1986, p. 79.

governments, equal opportunities committees and trade unions to carry out concerted information campaigns to create a proper awareness of the individual rights of all members of the labour force;

Whereas the Advisory Committee on Equal Opportunities for Women and Men, in its opinion of 20 June 1988, has unanimously recommended that there should be a recommendation and code of conduct on sexual harassment in the workplace covering harassment of both sexes;

Whereas the Commission in its action programme relating to the implementation of the Community Charter of Basic Social Rights for Workers undertook to examine the protection of workers and their dignity at work, having regard to the reports and recommendations prepared on various aspects of implementation of Community law;[1]

Whereas the Council, in its resolution of 29 May 1990 on the protection of the dignity of women and men at work,[2] affirms that conduct based on sex affecting the dignity of women and men at work, including conduct of superiors and colleagues, constitutes an intolerable violation of the dignity of workers or trainees, and calls on the Member States and the institutions and organs of the European Communities to develop positive measures designed to create a climate at work in which women and men respect one another's human integrity;

Whereas the Commission, in its third action programme on equal opportunities for women and men, 1991 to 1995, and pursuant to paragraph 3 (2) of the said Council resolution of 29 May 1990, resolved to draw up a code of conduct on the protection of the dignity of women and men at work,[3] based on experience and best practice in the Member States, to provide guidance on initiating and pursuing positive measures designed to create a climate at work in which women and men respect one another's human integrity; ▬

---

[1] COM(589) 568 final, 29.11.1989. For example, 'The dignity of women at work: A report on the problem of sexual harassment in the Member States of the European Communities', October 1987, by Michael Rubenstein (ISBN 92-825-8764-9).

[2] OJ C 157, 27.6.1990, p. 3.

[3] COM(90) 449 final, 6.11.1990.

Whereas the European Parliament, on 22 October 1991, adopted a resolution on the protection of the dignity of women and men at work;[1]

Whereas the Economic and Social Committee, on 30 October 1991, adopted an opinion on the protection of the dignity of women and men at work,[2]

RECOMMENDS AS FOLLOWS:

Article 1

It is recommended that the Member States take action to promote awareness that conduct of a sexual nature, or other conduct based on sex affecting the dignity of women and men at work, including conduct of superiors and colleagues, is unacceptable if:

(a) such conduct is unwanted, unreasonable and offensive to the recipient;

(b) a person's rejection of, or submission to, such conduct on the part of employers or workers (including superiors or colleagues) is used explicitly or implicitly as a basis for a decision which affects that person's access to vocational training, access to employment, continued employment, promotion, salary or any other employment decisions;

and/or

(c) such conduct creates an intimidating, hostile or humiliating work environment for the recipient;

and that such conduct may, in certain circumstances, be contrary to the principle of equal treatment within the meaning of Articles 3, 4 and 5 of directive 76/207/EEC.

---

[1] OJ C 305, 25.11.1991.
[2] OJ C 14, 20.1.1992.

Article 2

It is recommended that Member States take action, in the public sector, to implement the Commission's code of practice on the protection of the dignity of women and men at work, annexed hereto. The action of the Member States, in thus initiating and pursuing positive measures designed to create a climate at work in which women and men respect one another's human integrity, should serve as an example to the private sector.

Article 3

It is recommended that Member States encourage employers and employee representatives to develop measures to implement the Commission's code of practice on the protection of the dignity of women and men at work.

Article 4

Member States shall inform the Commission within three years of the date of this recommendation of the measures taken to give effect to it, in order to allow the Commission to draw up a report on all such measures. The Commission shall, within this period, ensure the widest possible circulation of the code of practice. The report should examine the degree of awareness of the Code, its perceived effectiveness, its degree of application and the extent of its use in collective bargaining between the social partners.

Article 5

This recommendation is addressed to the Member States.

Done at Brussels, 27 November 1991.

For the Commission
Vasso PAPANDREOU
Member of the Commission

(Information)

COUNCIL DECLARATION

of 19 December 1991 on the implementation of the Commission recommendation on the protection of the dignity of women and men at work, including the code of practice to combat sexual harassment (92/C 27/01)

THE COUNCIL OF THE EUROPEAN COMMUNITIES,

Considering that on 29 May 1990 the Council adopted a resolution on the protection of the dignity of women and men at work;[1]

Considering that on 27 November 1991 the Commission made a recommendation on the protection of the dignity of women and men at work,[2] to which is annexed a code of practice to combat sexual harassment;

Considering that on 21 May 1991 the Council adopted a resolution on the third medium-term Community action programme on equal opportunities for women and men (1991 to 1995);[3]

Considering that the European Parliament and the Economic and Social Committee have adopted respectively on 22 October 1991 a resolution[4] and on 30 October 1991 an opinion[5] on the protection of the dignity of women and men at work;

---

[1] OJ C 157, 27.6.1990, p. 3.
[2] See page 4 of this Official Journal.
[3] OJ C 142, 31.5.1991, p. 1.
[4] OJ C 305, 25.11.1991.
[5] OJ C 14, 20.1.1992.

Considering that the efforts already made to promote the integration of women on the labour market should be intensified and developed; considering that sexual harassment is a serious problem for many women working in the Community and an obstacle to their full integration into active life,

1. ENDORSES the general objective of the Commission recommendation;

2. INVITES THE MEMBER STATES to develop and implement coherent, integrated policies to prevent and combat sexual harassment at work, taking account of the Commission recommendation;

3. INVITES THE COMMISSION:

   (a) to promote an adequate exchange of information with a view to developing existing knowledge and experience in the Member States as regards the prevention and combating of sexual harassment at work;

   (b) to examine the assessment criteria for the evaluation of the effectiveness of the measures taken in the Member States, taking account of the criteria already in use there;

   (c) to endeavour to implement the criteria referred to in (b) when drawing up the report referred to in Article 4 of the Commission recommendation;

   (d) to submit the report referred to in Article 4 of the Commission recommendation to the European Parliament, the Council and the Economic and Social Committee not more than three years after the adoption of this declaration.

COUNCIL RESOLUTION

of 29 May 1990 on the protection of the dignity of women and men at work (90/C 157/02)

THE COUNCIL OF THE EUROPEAN COMMUNITIES,

Having regard to the Treaty establishing the European Economic Community,

Whereas unwanted conduct of a sexual nature, or other conduct based on sex affecting the dignity of women and men at work, including the conduct of superiors and colleagues, is unacceptable and may, in certain circumstances, be contrary to the principle of equal treatment within the meaning of Articles 3, 4 and 5 of Council Directive 76/207/EEC of 9 February 1976 on the implementation of the principle of equal treatment for men and women as regards access to employment, vocational training and promotion, and working conditions,[1] a view supported by case-law in some Member States;

Whereas, in accordance with the Council recommendation of 13 December 1984 on the promotion of positive action for women,[2] many Member States have carried out a variety of positive action measures and actions having a bearing, *inter alia*, on respect for the dignity of women at the workplace;

Whereas the European Parliament, in its resolution of 11 June 1986 on violence against women,[3] has called upon national authorities to strive to achieve a legal definition of sexual harassment and has called upon national governments, equal opportunities, committees and trade unions to carry out concerted information campaigns to create a proper awareness of the individual rights of all members of the labour force;

---

[1] OJ l 39, 14.2.1976, p. 40.
[2] OJ l 331, 19.12.1984, p. 34.
[3] OJ C 176, 14.7.1986, p. 79.

Whereas the Council is anxious to take account of the study which found that sexual harassment is a serious problem for many working women in the European Community and is an obstacle to the proper integration for women into the labour market;[1]

Whereas the Advisory Committee on Equal Opportunities between Women and Men, in its opinion of 20 June 1988, has unanimously recommended that there should be a recommendation and code of conduct on sexual harassment in the workplace covering harassment of both sexes,

1. AFFIRMS, that conduct of a sexual nature, or other conduct based on sex affecting the dignity of women and men at work, including conduct of superiors and colleagues, constitutes an intolerable violation of the dignity of workers or trainees and is unacceptable if:

(a) such conduct is unwanted, unreasonable and offensive to the recipient;

(b) a person's rejection of, or submission to, such conduct on the part of employers or workers (including superiors or colleagues) is used explicitly or implicitly as a basis for a decision which affects that person's access to vocational training, access to employment, continued employment, promotion, salary or any other employment decisions;

and/or

(c) such conduct creates an intimidating, hostile or humiliating work environment for the recipient;

2. CALLS ON the Member States to:

1. develop campaigns of information and awareness for employers and workers (including superiors and colleagues), taking account of the best practice which exists in various Member States, to counter unwanted conduct of a sexual

---

[1] 'The Dignity of Women at Work; Report on the problem of sexual harassment in the Member States of the European Communities, October 1987.' (ISBN 92-825-8764-9).

nature or other conduct based on sex affecting the dignity of women and men at work;

2. promote awareness that the conduct described in paragraph 1 may be, in certain circumstances, contrary to the principle of equal treatment within the meaning of Articles 3, 4 and 5 of Council Directive 76/207/EEC;

3. remind employers that they have a responsibility to seek to ensure that the work environment is free from:

   (a) unwanted conduct of a sexual nature or other conduct based on sex affecting the dignity of women and men at work;

   (b) victimization of a complainant or of a person wishing to give, or giving, evidence in the event of a complaint;

4. develop appropriate positive measures in accordance with national legislation in the public sector which may serve as an example to the private sector;

5. consider that both sides of industry, while respecting their autonomy and subjects to national traditions and practices, could examine in the context of the collective bargaining process the question of including appropriate clauses in agreements, aimed at achieving a work environment as described in paragraph 3.

3. CALLS ON THE Commission to

1. continue its efforts to inform and make aware employers, workers (including superiors and colleagues), lawyers and members of courts, tribunals and other competent authorities of the importance of the concept set out in paragraph 1 and of the fact that, in certain circumstances, failure to respect this concept may be contrary to the principle of equal treatment within the meaning of Articles 3, 4 and 5 of Directive 76/207/EEC;

2. draw up, by 1 July 1991, in consultation with both sides of industry and following consultation with the Member States

and national equal opportunities authorities, a code of conduct on the protection of the dignity of women and men at work which will provide guidance, based on examples and best practice in the Member States, on initiating and pursuing positive measures designed to create a climate at work in which women and men respect one another's human integrity.

4.   CALLS ON the institutions and organs of the European Communities also to

1.   respect the concept set out in paragraph 1,

2.   develop positive action measures, aimed at achieving a work environment as described in paragraph 2(3).

European Communites — Commission

How to combat sexual harassment at work: A guide to implementing the European Commission code of practice

Luxembourg: Office for Official Publications of the Communities

1993 — 104 pp. — 14.8 × 21 cm

ISBN 92-826-5225-4